LangGraph AI Agents

A Hands-on Guide to Autonomous AI System Development

James Wiglow

Copyright Page

Disclaimer:
The author and publisher have made every effort to ensure the accuracy of the information provided in this book. However, this book is not intended as professional advice, and readers should consult with professionals in relevant fields where appropriate.

Table of Contents

Preface

About the Author

Welcome to *"LangGraph AI Agents: A Hands-on Guide to Autonomous AI System Development."* My name is [Your Name], and I have dedicated the past [number] years to the field of artificial intelligence and machine learning. With a background in [Your Background – e.g., computer science, software engineering], I have worked extensively on developing and deploying AI systems across various industries, including [mention industries, e.g., healthcare, finance, logistics].

Throughout my career, I have been particularly fascinated by the potential of autonomous AI agents to revolutionize how we interact with technology and solve complex problems. My experience spans from designing intelligent systems using LangGraph to managing multi-agent frameworks that enhance operational efficiency and decision-making processes. This book is a culmination of my practical knowledge, research, and passion for making advanced AI accessible to developers, engineers, and enthusiasts alike.

Purpose of the Book

The primary goal of this book is to provide a comprehensive, hands-on guide to building and managing autonomous AI agent systems using LangGraph. As AI continues to evolve, the demand for robust, scalable, and intelligent systems grows exponentially. However, many practitioners find it challenging to navigate the complexities involved in developing such systems.

This book aims to bridge that gap by offering clear, step-by-step instructions, practical examples, and in-depth explanations of key concepts. Whether you're a seasoned developer looking to enhance your skills or a newcomer eager to dive into the world of autonomous AI agents, this guide is designed to equip you with the knowledge and tools necessary to succeed.

Who Should Read This Book

"LangGraph AI Agents: A Hands-on Guide to Autonomous AI System Development" is tailored for a diverse audience, including:

- **Developers and Engineers**: Individuals with a programming background who wish to integrate autonomous AI agents into their applications.
- **AI Enthusiasts and Researchers**: Those interested in exploring the capabilities and advancements of AI agents within the LangGraph framework.
- **IT Professionals and Managers**: Professionals overseeing AI projects who need a comprehensive understanding of developing and managing autonomous systems.
- **Students and Educators**: Academics and learners seeking a practical resource to complement their studies in artificial intelligence and machine learning.

Regardless of your current expertise level, this book is structured to guide you from foundational concepts to advanced implementations, ensuring a thorough understanding of autonomous AI system development.

How to Use This Book

To maximize the benefits of this guide, consider the following approaches:

1. **Sequential Reading**: Start from the beginning and progress through each chapter in order. The book is structured to build upon previously introduced concepts, ensuring a logical and comprehensive learning experience.
2. **Project-Based Learning**: Engage actively with the hands-on projects and exercises provided at the end of each chapter. Implementing these projects will reinforce your understanding and provide practical experience in building AI agents.
3. **Reference Guide**: Use the book as a reference tool. If you encounter specific challenges or need to revisit certain topics, the detailed Table of Contents and Index will help you locate the necessary information quickly.
4. **Interactive Learning**: Take advantage of the accompanying code repositories and online resources. Experimenting with the provided code examples and customizing them for your projects will deepen your practical knowledge.
5. **Community Engagement**: Join discussions in the book's dedicated online forum or community platform (if available). Collaborating with fellow readers can provide additional insights, support, and inspiration for your AI projects.

Acknowledgments

Creating this book has been a journey filled with learning, collaboration, and support from numerous individuals and organizations. I would like to extend my heartfelt gratitude to:

- **My Mentors and Colleagues**: Your guidance, feedback, and encouragement have been invaluable throughout this project.
- **The LangGraph Community**: Your contributions, discussions, and shared knowledge have greatly enriched the content of this book.
- **Beta Readers and Testers**: Thank you for your critical reviews and constructive feedback, which have helped refine and enhance the quality of this guide.
- **Family and Friends**: Your unwavering support and understanding have been the backbone of this endeavor.
- **OpenAI and Other Technology Providers**: For providing the tools and platforms that made the development and deployment of AI agents possible.

Lastly, I dedicate this book to all the aspiring AI developers and enthusiasts who are eager to push the boundaries of what's possible with autonomous AI systems. May this guide empower you to build innovative solutions and contribute to the ever-evolving landscape of artificial intelligence.

Chapter 1: Introduction to Autonomous AI Systems

Welcome to the first chapter of *"LangGraph AI Agents: A Hands-on Guide to Autonomous AI System Development."* In this chapter, we will lay the foundation for understanding autonomous AI systems and the role of LangGraph in developing these intelligent agents. We will explore the definition and importance of autonomous AI agents, their historical evolution, an overview of LangGraph, various applications across industries, ethical and social implications, and finally, the structure of this book to guide your learning journey.

1.1 Understanding Autonomous AI Agents

Definition and Importance

Autonomous AI agents are intelligent systems designed to perform tasks or make decisions without human intervention. These agents operate based on predefined rules, learning algorithms, or a combination of both, enabling them to adapt to changing environments and optimize their performance over time.

Key Characteristics of Autonomous AI Agents:

1. **Autonomy:** Ability to operate independently without constant human guidance.
2. **Adaptability:** Capability to adjust behaviors based on new information or changes in the environment.
3. **Goal-Oriented:** Focused on achieving specific objectives or completing designated tasks.
4. **Learning Capability:** Utilizes machine learning techniques to improve performance through experience.
5. **Interactivity:** Engages with other systems, agents, or users to perform complex tasks.

Importance of Autonomous AI Agents:

- **Efficiency:** Automate repetitive and time-consuming tasks, allowing humans to focus on more strategic activities.

- **Scalability:** Handle large volumes of tasks simultaneously without a decrease in performance.
- **Consistency:** Provide reliable and uniform outcomes, minimizing human error.
- **24/7 Operation:** Function continuously without the need for breaks or downtime.
- **Cost-Effectiveness:** Reduce operational costs by minimizing the need for human labor in certain areas.

Examples of Autonomous AI Agents in Daily Life:

- **Virtual Assistants:** Siri, Alexa, and Google Assistant help users manage tasks, answer questions, and control smart devices.
- **Autonomous Vehicles:** Self-driving cars navigate roads, avoid obstacles, and make real-time driving decisions.
- **Robotic Process Automation (RPA):** Software bots automate business processes like data entry, invoicing, and customer service.

Historical Evolution of AI Agents

The journey of autonomous AI agents has been marked by significant milestones that have shaped their current capabilities and applications.

Early Beginnings:

- **1950s-1960s:** The concept of artificial intelligence (AI) was introduced, with pioneers like Alan Turing and John McCarthy laying the groundwork for machine intelligence.
- **1966:** ELIZA, one of the first chatbots, was developed by Joseph Weizenbaum, simulating human conversation.

Advancements in AI Research:

- **1970s-1980s:** Development of expert systems, which mimicked the decision-making abilities of human experts in specific domains.
- **1997:** IBM's Deep Blue defeated world chess champion Garry Kasparov, showcasing the potential of AI in strategic game-playing.

Rise of Machine Learning and Deep Learning:

- **2000s:** Emergence of machine learning algorithms that enabled systems to learn from data and improve over time.

- **2010s:** Breakthroughs in deep learning led to significant advancements in natural language processing, computer vision, and autonomous systems.

Modern Autonomous AI Agents:

- **2016:** Google's DeepMind developed AlphaGo, which defeated a world champion Go player, demonstrating complex decision-making and strategic planning.
- **2020s:** Integration of AI agents into various industries, from healthcare and finance to transportation and entertainment, driven by advancements in LangGraph and similar frameworks.

Table 1.1: Milestones in the Evolution of AI Agents

Year	Milestone	Description
1950	Introduction of AI Concept	Alan Turing proposes the Turing Test to evaluate machine intelligence.
1966	Development of ELIZA	Joseph Weizenbaum creates one of the first natural language processing programs.
1972	MYCIN Expert System	An early AI system designed to diagnose blood infections.
1997	Deep Blue vs. Garry Kasparov	IBM's chess-playing computer defeats the world champion.
2016	AlphaGo Defeats Lee Sedol	DeepMind's AI system wins against a top Go player, highlighting strategic AI.
2020	Rise of Autonomous Vehicles	Significant advancements in self-driving car technology.
2023	Launch of LangGraph Framework	Introduction of LangGraph for building and managing autonomous AI agents.

1.2 Overview of LangGraph

What is LangGraph?

LangGraph is a cutting-edge framework designed to simplify the development, deployment, and management of autonomous AI agents. It provides developers with a robust set of tools and libraries that facilitate the creation of intelligent agents capable of performing complex tasks across various domains.

Key Components of LangGraph:

1. **Agent Builder:** A user-friendly interface for designing and configuring AI agents without extensive coding.
2. **Task Scheduler:** Manages the execution of tasks, ensuring that agents operate efficiently and effectively.
3. **Communication Hub:** Facilitates seamless interaction between multiple agents and external systems.
4. **Learning Module:** Integrates machine learning algorithms to enable agents to learn and adapt from data.
5. **Monitoring Dashboard:** Provides real-time insights into agent performance, system health, and operational metrics.

Benefits of Using LangGraph:

- **Ease of Use:** Streamlines the agent development process with intuitive tools and pre-built components.
- **Scalability:** Supports the deployment of large-scale agent systems capable of handling numerous tasks simultaneously.
- **Flexibility:** Compatible with various programming languages and can be integrated with existing systems and technologies.
- **Robustness:** Ensures reliability and stability through built-in error handling and performance optimization features.
- **Community Support:** Backed by an active community of developers and continuous updates to incorporate the latest advancements in AI.

Key Features and Capabilities

LangGraph stands out in the realm of AI frameworks due to its comprehensive feature set and capabilities that empower developers to build sophisticated autonomous systems with ease.

1. Modular Architecture:

- **Plugin System:** Allows developers to extend LangGraph's functionality by integrating custom plugins tailored to specific needs.
- **Microservices Integration:** Facilitates the connection of LangGraph agents with microservices for enhanced modularity and scalability.

2. Advanced Machine Learning Integration:

- **Pre-trained Models:** Access to a library of pre-trained machine learning models that can be easily incorporated into agents.
- **Custom Training Pipelines:** Tools for training and fine-tuning models based on specific datasets and requirements.

3. Natural Language Processing (NLP):

- **Language Understanding:** Enables agents to comprehend and process human language effectively.
- **Dialogue Management:** Manages conversational flows, making interactions with agents more natural and intuitive.

4. Real-Time Data Processing:

- **Streaming Capabilities:** Allows agents to handle real-time data streams, making them suitable for applications like financial trading or monitoring systems.
- **Event-Driven Architecture:** Enables agents to respond promptly to events and changes in their environment.

5. Robust Security Features:

- **Authentication and Authorization:** Ensures that only authorized users and systems can interact with agents.
- **Data Encryption:** Protects sensitive data through encryption both at rest and in transit.

6. Comprehensive Monitoring and Analytics:

- **Performance Metrics:** Tracks key performance indicators (KPIs) to assess agent efficiency and effectiveness.
- **Alerting Systems:** Notifies administrators of any anomalies or issues in real-time, enabling prompt resolution.

7. User-Friendly Interface:

- **Dashboard:** An intuitive dashboard for managing agents, viewing analytics, and configuring system settings.

- **Visualization Tools:** Provides visual representations of agent workflows, data flows, and system architecture for better understanding and management.

8. Integration with Third-Party Services:

- **API Support:** Facilitates integration with various third-party APIs, enhancing the capabilities of autonomous agents.
- **Cloud Compatibility:** Compatible with major cloud platforms like AWS, Azure, and Google Cloud, allowing for flexible deployment options.

Table 1.2: Key Features of LangGraph

Feature	Description
Modular Architecture	Plugin system and microservices integration for flexibility and scalability.
Advanced ML Integration	Pre-trained models and custom training pipelines for enhanced learning.
Natural Language Processing	Language understanding and dialogue management for better interactions.
Real-Time Data Processing	Streaming capabilities and event-driven architecture for dynamic environments.
Robust Security Features	Authentication, authorization, and data encryption for secure operations.
Comprehensive Monitoring	Performance metrics and alerting systems for proactive management.
User-Friendly Interface	Intuitive dashboard and visualization tools for easy management.
Third-Party Integration	API support and cloud compatibility for enhanced functionality.

1.3 Applications of Autonomous AI Systems

Autonomous AI systems have a wide array of applications across various industries. Their ability to operate independently, process large amounts of data, and make informed decisions makes them invaluable in solving complex problems and improving operational efficiency.

Industry Use Cases

1. **Healthcare:**
   - **Medical Diagnostics:** AI agents assist in diagnosing diseases by analyzing medical images and patient data.
   - **Personalized Treatment Plans:** Develop tailored treatment strategies based on individual patient profiles and medical histories.
   - **Administrative Automation:** Automate tasks like scheduling appointments, managing patient records, and processing insurance claims.
2. **Finance:**
   - **Fraud Detection:** Identify and prevent fraudulent transactions by analyzing patterns and anomalies in financial data.
   - **Algorithmic Trading:** Execute trades at optimal times based on real-time market data and predictive analytics.
   - **Customer Service:** Deploy AI-powered chatbots to handle customer inquiries, provide financial advice, and manage accounts.
3. **Transportation:**
   - **Autonomous Vehicles:** Develop self-driving cars and drones that navigate roads and airspace without human intervention.
   - **Traffic Management:** Optimize traffic flow in cities by analyzing data from various sources and controlling traffic signals.
   - **Logistics and Supply Chain:** Automate inventory management, route planning, and delivery scheduling to enhance efficiency.
4. **Retail:**
   - **Personalized Shopping Experiences:** Recommend products to customers based on their browsing history and preferences.
   - **Inventory Management:** Monitor stock levels in real-time and automate restocking processes.
   - **Customer Support:** Implement AI agents to handle customer queries, process orders, and manage returns.
5. **Manufacturing:**
   - **Predictive Maintenance:** Monitor machinery for signs of wear and predict maintenance needs before failures occur.
   - **Quality Control:** Inspect products for defects using computer vision and machine learning algorithms.

- o **Process Optimization:** Analyze production data to identify bottlenecks and optimize manufacturing processes.
6. **Energy:**
   - o **Smart Grid Management:** Optimize energy distribution and consumption by analyzing real-time data from the grid.
   - o **Renewable Energy Forecasting:** Predict energy generation from renewable sources like solar and wind to balance supply and demand.
   - o **Energy Efficiency:** Develop strategies to reduce energy consumption in buildings and industrial facilities.

Real-World Examples

1. **AI-Powered Customer Support:**
   - o **Example:** A major e-commerce platform deploys AI agents to handle customer inquiries, process orders, and manage returns. These agents provide instant responses, reducing wait times and improving customer satisfaction.
2. **Autonomous Delivery Drones:**
   - o **Example:** A logistics company uses autonomous drones to deliver packages to remote or congested areas. The drones navigate using AI algorithms, ensuring timely and efficient deliveries without human intervention.
3. **Predictive Maintenance in Manufacturing:**
   - o **Example:** A car manufacturing plant implements AI agents to monitor machinery performance in real-time. By analyzing data from sensors, the agents predict when maintenance is needed, preventing unexpected downtime and reducing maintenance costs.
4. **Smart Traffic Management Systems:**
   - o **Example:** A smart city employs AI agents to manage traffic signals based on real-time traffic data. This reduces congestion, minimizes travel times, and lowers emissions by optimizing traffic flow.
5. **Personalized Healthcare Assistants:**
   - o **Example:** Hospitals use AI-powered virtual assistants to provide personalized health advice to patients. These agents analyze patient data and medical histories to offer tailored recommendations, improving patient outcomes and enhancing care quality.

Table 1.3: Applications of Autonomous AI Systems Across Industries

Industry	Application	Description
Healthcare	Medical Diagnostics	AI agents analyze medical images and data to assist in disease diagnosis.
Finance	Fraud Detection	Identify and prevent fraudulent transactions by analyzing financial data.
Transportation	Autonomous Vehicles	Develop self-driving cars and drones for navigation without human input.
Retail	Personalized Shopping Experiences	Recommend products to customers based on their preferences and behavior.
Manufacturing	Predictive Maintenance	Monitor machinery to predict and schedule maintenance before failures occur.
Energy	Smart Grid Management	Optimize energy distribution and consumption using real-time data analysis.

1.4 Ethical and Social Implications

As autonomous AI systems become more integrated into various aspects of society, it is crucial to address the ethical and social implications associated with their deployment and use. Ensuring that AI agents are developed and managed responsibly is essential for fostering trust, fairness, and accountability.

Ethical AI Development

Ethical AI development involves designing and implementing AI systems that adhere to moral principles and societal values. Key considerations include:

1. **Transparency:** Ensuring that AI systems operate in an open and understandable manner. This includes making the decision-making processes of AI agents clear to users and stakeholders.
2. **Accountability:** Establishing clear lines of responsibility for the actions and decisions made by AI agents. This involves determining who is liable for any negative outcomes resulting from AI operations.

3. **Fairness:** Preventing bias and ensuring that AI systems treat all individuals and groups equitably. This includes addressing any disparities in how AI agents interact with different demographics.
4. **Privacy:** Protecting the personal and sensitive data that AI agents may collect and process. Implementing robust data protection measures to prevent unauthorized access and misuse.
5. **Beneficence:** Designing AI systems that promote the well-being of individuals and society. Ensuring that AI agents contribute positively and do not cause harm.

Best Practices for Ethical AI Development:

- **Inclusive Design:** Involve diverse teams in the development process to minimize biases and ensure that AI systems cater to a broad range of users.
- **Ethical Audits:** Regularly assess AI systems for compliance with ethical standards and guidelines.
- **User Consent:** Obtain explicit consent from users before collecting and using their data.
- **Explainability:** Develop AI agents that can provide understandable explanations for their decisions and actions.

Bias Mitigation

Bias in AI occurs when an AI system produces prejudiced outcomes due to biased training data or flawed algorithms. Bias can lead to unfair treatment of individuals or groups, reinforcing existing societal inequalities.

Sources of Bias:

1. **Training Data:** If the data used to train AI agents contains biases, these biases can be learned and perpetuated by the agents.
2. **Algorithm Design:** Algorithms that do not account for fairness can inadvertently introduce or amplify biases.
3. **User Interaction:** The way users interact with AI agents can introduce biases, especially if the agents adapt based on user input without proper safeguards.

Strategies for Mitigating Bias:

1. **Diverse Training Data:** Ensure that the data used for training AI agents is representative of all relevant populations and scenarios.

2. **Bias Detection Tools:** Utilize tools and techniques to identify and measure bias in AI systems during the development and testing phases.
3. **Algorithmic Fairness:** Implement fairness-aware algorithms that aim to produce equitable outcomes across different groups.
4. **Continuous Monitoring:** Regularly monitor AI agents in operation to detect and address any emerging biases.

Example of Bias Mitigation:

Consider an AI-powered hiring assistant that screens job applications. If the training data predominantly includes successful candidates from a particular gender or ethnicity, the AI agent may develop a bias against other groups. To mitigate this, developers should:

- **Use Balanced Data:** Incorporate diverse applicant data that reflects various genders, ethnicities, and backgrounds.
- **Audit Decisions:** Regularly review the hiring decisions made by the AI agent to identify any patterns of bias.
- **Adjust Algorithms:** Modify the decision-making algorithms to ensure they promote fairness and do not disadvantage any group.

Impact on Society

The widespread adoption of autonomous AI systems has profound implications for society, influencing various aspects of daily life, work, and governance.

Positive Impacts:

1. **Increased Efficiency:** Automation of tasks leads to faster and more accurate outcomes, enhancing productivity across industries.
2. **Innovation:** AI-driven solutions foster innovation, enabling the development of new products, services, and business models.
3. **Accessibility:** AI agents can improve accessibility for individuals with disabilities by providing assistive technologies and personalized support.
4. **Healthcare Advancements:** Enhanced diagnostics, personalized medicine, and efficient administrative processes contribute to better healthcare outcomes.

Negative Impacts:

1. **Job Displacement:** Automation may lead to the displacement of jobs, particularly in sectors reliant on routine and repetitive tasks.
2. **Privacy Concerns:** The collection and processing of vast amounts of data by AI agents can infringe on individuals' privacy rights.
3. **Security Risks:** Autonomous AI systems can be vulnerable to cyberattacks, leading to potential misuse or exploitation.
4. **Ethical Dilemmas:** Decisions made by AI agents in critical areas, such as healthcare or criminal justice, raise ethical questions about accountability and fairness.

Balancing the Impacts:

To maximize the benefits and minimize the drawbacks of autonomous AI systems, it is essential to:

- **Implement Regulatory Frameworks:** Establish laws and guidelines that govern the development and deployment of AI technologies.
- **Promote Ethical Standards:** Encourage adherence to ethical principles in AI research and application.
- **Foster Public Awareness:** Educate the public about the capabilities and limitations of AI agents to build informed consent and trust.
- **Support Workforce Transition:** Provide training and education programs to help workers adapt to the changing job landscape influenced by AI automation.

1.5 Structure of the Book

Understanding the structure of this book will help you navigate through the content effectively and make the most of the learning opportunities it offers.

How the Content is Organized

This book is meticulously structured to guide you from the foundational concepts of autonomous AI systems to advanced implementations using LangGraph. Each chapter builds upon the previous ones, ensuring a logical progression of knowledge and skills.

Key Organizational Principles:

1. **Sequential Learning:** Chapters are arranged in a sequence that starts with basic concepts and gradually advances to more complex topics.

2. **Modular Structure:** Each chapter focuses on specific aspects of autonomous AI system development, allowing you to delve into areas of interest independently.
3. **Practical Focus:** Emphasis on hands-on projects, real-world examples, and practical applications to reinforce theoretical knowledge.
4. **Comprehensive Coverage:** Covers a wide range of topics, from agent design and machine learning integration to deployment, security, and ethical considerations.

Chapter Breakdown:

- **Chapters 1-3:** Introduction to autonomous AI agents, understanding LangGraph, and building basic AI agents.
- **Chapters 4-6:** Advanced agent behaviors, multi-agent systems, and reinforcement learning.
- **Chapters 7-8:** Integrating external systems and APIs, and deployment and scaling of AI agents.
- **Chapters 9-10:** Security and compliance, and observability and monitoring.
- **Chapters 11-14:** Optimization and performance tuning, case studies, best practices, and future trends.
- **Chapter 15:** Appendices with additional resources.
- **Chapter 16:** Exercises and projects to reinforce learning.

Learning Path Overview

To facilitate an effective learning experience, follow this recommended path through the book:

1. **Start with Chapter 1:** Gain a comprehensive understanding of autonomous AI systems, their significance, and the role of LangGraph.
2. **Proceed to Chapter 2:** Set up your development environment and get acquainted with LangGraph's architecture and basic functionalities.
3. **Move to Chapter 3:** Begin building your first AI agents, focusing on foundational skills and simple implementations.
4. **Advance to Chapters 4-6:** Explore advanced behaviors, multi-agent systems, and reinforcement learning to enhance your AI agents' capabilities.

5. **Continue with Chapters 7-8:** Learn how to integrate external systems and APIs, and understand the deployment and scaling processes for AI agents.
6. **Study Chapters 9-10:** Focus on securing your AI systems and implementing effective monitoring and observability practices.
7. **Deepen Your Knowledge with Chapters 11-14:** Optimize and fine-tune your AI agents, analyze real-world applications, adopt best practices, and stay informed about future trends.
8. **Utilize Chapter 15:** Refer to the appendices for additional resources, troubleshooting, and a comprehensive glossary.
9. **Engage with Chapter 16:** Apply your knowledge through hands-on projects, practice problems, and advanced challenges to solidify your understanding and skills.

Visual Learning Tools:

- **Flowcharts and Diagrams:** Each chapter includes visual aids to help you grasp complex concepts and system architectures.
- **Code Examples:** Practical code snippets and complete examples demonstrate how to implement various features and functionalities.
- **Screenshots:** Step-by-step instructions are supported by screenshots to guide you through processes and implementations.

Interactive Learning:

- **Hands-On Projects:** Engage with projects that simulate real-world scenarios, allowing you to apply what you've learned in a practical context.
- **Practice Problems:** Test your understanding with questions designed to reinforce key concepts and challenge your knowledge.
- **Community Support:** Access online forums or discussion groups to interact with fellow readers, share insights, and seek assistance when needed.

Final Thoughts:

This book is designed to be your comprehensive guide to developing and managing autonomous AI systems using LangGraph. By following the structured learning path and engaging with the practical examples and projects, you will gain the expertise needed to build sophisticated AI agents that can operate independently and efficiently in various environments.

As you progress through the chapters, remember to:

- **Stay Curious:** Continuously explore new concepts and technologies related to AI and LangGraph.
- **Practice Regularly:** Apply what you learn through hands-on projects to reinforce your understanding.
- **Seek Feedback:** Engage with the community and seek feedback to improve your skills and knowledge.
- **Stay Updated:** Keep abreast of the latest advancements in AI to ensure your skills remain relevant and cutting-edge.

Embark on this journey to master the art of autonomous AI system development with LangGraph, and unlock the potential to create intelligent agents that can transform industries and enhance our daily lives.

Chapter 2: Getting Started with LangGraph

In this chapter, we will guide you through setting up your development environment for LangGraph, an essential step before diving into the practical creation of autonomous AI agents. By the end of this chapter, you will have a clear understanding of how to set up the tools, navigate LangGraph's architecture, create your first AI agent, and get hands-on experience running and testing it. Let's get started!

2.1 Setting Up Your Development Environment

Before you can begin building AI agents using LangGraph, you need to set up the appropriate development environment. This section covers the required tools and software, followed by a step-by-step installation guide.

Required Tools and Software

To get started, you need to install the following tools and software:

1. **Programming Language: Python**
   o LangGraph is primarily designed for Python, so you'll need Python 3.7 or later. Python is a versatile language that offers libraries and tools suitable for building AI systems.

   Download Python: Python Official Website

2. **LangGraph Framework**
   o LangGraph itself is a Python package that you will install using `pip`, Python's package manager. LangGraph provides a set of modules to help you design, deploy, and manage autonomous AI agents.

   Install LangGraph: You will install the LangGraph library from PyPI (Python Package Index). Make sure you have Python installed first.

```
pip install langgraph
```

3. **IDE or Code Editor**
   o A code editor or Integrated Development Environment (IDE) is essential for writing your Python code. Commonly used editors include:
      - **VSCode**: Lightweight and highly customizable.
      - **PyCharm**: Excellent for Python development with built-in debugging and testing features.

   Download VSCode: Visual Studio Code

   Download PyCharm: PyCharm Official Website

4. **Version Control (Git)**
   o Git is necessary for managing your code versions and collaborating with others. You can create repositories on platforms like GitHub or GitLab to store your projects.

   Download Git: Git Official Website

5. **Package Management (pip and virtualenv)**
   o **pip** is the Python package manager that will help you install external libraries.
   o **virtualenv** is recommended to manage project-specific dependencies in isolated environments, avoiding conflicts with other Python projects.

   To install virtualenv, run:

   ```
   pip install virtualenv
   ```

6. **Other Python Libraries**
   o Depending on the complexity of your AI agents, you may need additional libraries such as:
      - **NumPy** for numerical operations.
      - **Pandas** for data manipulation.
      - **TensorFlow** or **PyTorch** for deep learning.

   Install these with:

   ```
   pip install numpy pandas tensorflow
   ```

Installation Guide

1. **Step 1: Install Python**
   - Visit the Python official website and download the latest version for your operating system.
   - Run the installer and ensure that you check the option to **Add Python to PATH** during installation.
2. **Step 2: Install LangGraph**
   - Open your terminal or command prompt and run the following command to install LangGraph:
3. `pip install langgraph`
4. **Step 3: Set Up Virtual Environment**
   - Create a new directory for your project:
5. `mkdir my_ai_agent_project`
6. `cd my_ai_agent_project`
   - Create a virtual environment:
7. `python -m venv venv`
   - Activate the virtual environment:
      - **Windows:**
   - `.\venv\Scripts\activate`
      - **Mac/Linux:**
   - `source venv/bin/activate`
8. **Step 4: Install Required Libraries**
   - With the virtual environment activated, install any additional libraries you need:
9. `pip install numpy pandas tensorflow`
10. **Step 5: Verify Installation**
   - Ensure everything is set up correctly by running a simple Python script:
11. `import langgraph`
12. `print("LangGraph installed successfully!")`

If the installation is successful, you should see the message "LangGraph installed successfully!"

2.2 Introduction to LangGraph Architecture

LangGraph provides a modular architecture that allows developers to build scalable, autonomous AI agents quickly and efficiently. In this section, we will discuss the core components of LangGraph and the system requirements for running it.

Core Components

LangGraph is designed to streamline the process of building AI agents, offering the following core components:

1. **Agent Builder**:
   o The Agent Builder is a high-level interface for defining and configuring your agents. It allows you to specify behaviors, goals, and actions without requiring complex programming.
   o It provides templates for common agent types (e.g., customer service agents, data processing agents) that you can customize for your needs.
2. **Task Scheduler**:
   o This component manages the execution of tasks assigned to the AI agents. It ensures that agents complete their tasks in an orderly and efficient manner by handling time-based events, priority queues, and task dependencies.
3. **Learning Module**:
   o The Learning Module integrates machine learning algorithms that allow agents to improve their decision-making over time by learning from past experiences or data. This module can support supervised learning, reinforcement learning, or other AI methodologies.
4. **Communication Hub**:
   o The Communication Hub enables agents to communicate with each other and with external systems. It uses protocols like RESTful APIs and WebSockets to facilitate real-time data exchange between agents or systems.
5. **Monitoring Dashboard**:
   o This provides a graphical interface to monitor the performance of your agents. You can view metrics such as task completion rate, resource usage, and decision-making accuracy in real-time.

System Requirements

To run LangGraph efficiently, ensure your system meets the following requirements:

- **Operating System**: LangGraph is compatible with Windows, macOS, and Linux.

- **RAM**: Minimum 8 GB RAM (16 GB recommended for complex models).
- **Processor**: Intel Core i5 or higher (Intel Core i7 or equivalent recommended).
- **Storage**: At least 20 GB of free disk space for installation and storing agent data.
- **Python**: Python 3.7 or higher.
- **Libraries**: As mentioned earlier, make sure to install essential libraries like LangGraph, NumPy, TensorFlow, etc.

2.3 First Steps: Creating Your First AI Agent

Now that your environment is set up and you understand LangGraph's architecture, it's time to create your first AI agent. In this section, we will walk you through creating a basic agent, running it, and testing its functionality.

Basic Agent Creation

Let's create a simple agent that can execute tasks autonomously. Here's the basic code to create a simple agent:

```
import langgraph

# Define a simple AI agent
class SimpleAgent(langgraph.Agent):
    def __init__(self, name):
        super().__init__(name)
        self.goal = "Complete Task"

    def perform_task(self):
        print(f"{self.name} is performing the task!")
        # Simulating task completion
        self.complete_task()

# Initialize and run the agent
if __name__ == "__main__":
    agent = SimpleAgent(name="TaskMaster")
    agent.perform_task()
```

In this code:

- **langgraph.Agent**: The `Agent` class from LangGraph is inherited to define a new agent.
- **perform_task()**: This method simulates the agent performing a simple task, such as printing a message and marking the task as complete.

Running and Testing Your Agent

To run and test the agent, follow these steps:

1. **Create a new Python file** (e.g., `simple_agent.py`) and copy the code provided above.
2. **Run the file** in your terminal or IDE:
3. `python simple_agent.py`
4. You should see the following output:
5. `TaskMaster is performing the task!`

This demonstrates that your agent is functioning as expected, performing a task autonomously.

2.4 Understanding LangGraph's API

LangGraph provides a well-documented API that allows you to interact with and control your agents. In this section, we'll cover the key API endpoints and methods, as well as how to handle authentication and security.

Key Endpoints and Methods

LangGraph's API enables you to perform various operations, such as creating agents, managing tasks, and monitoring performance.

1. **Creating an Agent**:
   - **Endpoint**: `/agents/create`
   - **Method**: `POST`
   - **Parameters**: `name`, `goal`, `type`
   - **Description**: Creates a new agent with a specified goal and type.

Example (Python):

```python
response = langgraph.create_agent(name="TaskMaster",
goal="Complete Task", type="SimpleAgent")
print(response)
```

2. **Task Management**:
   o **Endpoint**: /tasks/perform
   o **Method**: POST
   o **Parameters**: agent_id, task
   o **Description**: Assigns a task to an agent.

Example (Python):

```python
task_response =
langgraph.perform_task(agent_id="12345", task="Perform
action A")
print(task_response)
```

3. **Monitoring Agent Performance**:
   o **Endpoint**: /agents/{agent_id}/status
   o **Method**: GET
   o **Description**: Retrieves the status of a specific agent.

Example (Python):

```python
agent_status =
langgraph.get_agent_status(agent_id="12345")
print(agent_status)
```

Authentication and Security

To ensure that only authorized users can interact with LangGraph agents, the API uses **API keys** for authentication.

1. **Generating an API Key**:
   o Log in to your LangGraph account.
   o Navigate to the **API Keys** section and generate a new key.
   o Store the key securely and never share it publicly.
2. **Using the API Key**:
   o When making API requests, pass the API key as part of the header.

Example (Python):

```python
import requests

headers = {
    "Authorization": "Bearer YOUR_API_KEY"
}

response =
requests.get("https://api.langgraph.com/agents/12345/st
atus", headers=headers)
print(response.json())
```

Important: Always keep your API keys secure. Do not expose them in public repositories or share them with unauthorized parties.

Summary

In this chapter, we've covered:

- **Setting up your development environment**: Installing Python, LangGraph, and the necessary tools.
- **LangGraph's architecture**: Key components that make LangGraph efficient for building autonomous AI systems.
- **Creating your first AI agent**: A simple example of agent creation, running, and testing.
- **LangGraph's API**: Key API methods for creating agents, managing tasks, and monitoring performance, along with authentication best practices.

By now, you should be comfortable with setting up LangGraph and creating basic agents. In the next chapter, we will explore how to build more sophisticated agents and leverage LangGraph's powerful features to design intelligent, autonomous systems.

Chapter 3: Building Basic AI Agents

In this chapter, we will guide you through the process of building your first **basic AI agent**. We'll cover the essential steps for designing agent workflows, implementing simple decision-making, managing agent states, and debugging/testing your agents. By the end of this chapter, you'll have the skills necessary to create functional AI agents capable of performing autonomous tasks based on workflows, rules, and decisions.

3.1 Designing Agent Workflows

Before building an AI agent, it is important to understand the workflow that the agent will follow. A **workflow** defines the sequence of tasks or operations the agent will carry out to achieve a goal. Designing an effective workflow ensures that the agent can execute its tasks efficiently and autonomously.

Defining Objectives and Goals

Every AI agent should have clear **objectives** and **goals**. The **goal** represents the desired outcome, while the **objectives** are the intermediate tasks the agent needs to complete in order to reach that outcome. Defining these clearly is crucial for the agent's behavior.

Example Goal and Objectives for a Customer Support Agent:

- **Goal:** Resolve customer inquiries by providing accurate and helpful information.
- **Objectives:**
    1. Understand the customer's query.
    2. Search for relevant data or FAQs.
    3. Provide the answer or escalate if needed.

Key Elements in Goal Definition:

1. **Specificity**: Goals should be specific and measurable. For example, a goal of "assist customers" can be unclear, whereas "resolve 80% of customer queries without escalation" is specific.

2. **Achievability**: Ensure that the goal is attainable within the context of the agent's capabilities.
3. **Relevance**: The goal must align with the purpose of the agent.

Workflow Diagrams and Flowcharts

Creating a **workflow diagram** or **flowchart** is an effective way to visualize the steps an agent will take to achieve its goal. These diagrams help clarify the sequence of actions and decision points in the agent's operation.

Basic Customer Support Agent Workflow:

1. **Start**: The agent receives a customer query.
2. **Understand Query**: The agent processes the input to understand the nature of the query.
3. **Search Knowledge Base**: Based on the query, the agent searches a knowledge base or FAQ repository for a relevant response.
4. **Provide Response**: If an answer is found, the agent provides it to the customer.
5. **Escalate Query**: If no relevant information is found, the agent escalates the query to a human support agent.
6. **End**: The process is complete.

Flowchart Example:

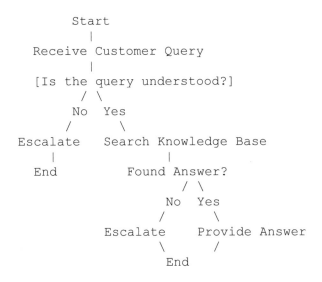

Creating a flowchart like this helps the developer to define each step the agent will take and ensures that the agent's behavior is well-structured and logical.

3.2 Implementing Simple Decision-Making

Once the workflow is defined, the next step is to implement the agent's decision-making process. Decision-making is how the agent decides which action to take next based on the available data and inputs.

Conditional Logic in Agents

The most basic form of decision-making in AI agents is **conditional logic**. This allows agents to choose different paths based on specific conditions or criteria. It can be implemented using `if-else` statements or more complex decision trees, depending on the needs of the agent.

Example: Basic Conditional Logic for a Customer Support Agent:

Let's implement the workflow from the previous section with simple decision-making using Python.

```python
class CustomerSupportAgent:
    def __init__(self):
        self.knowledge_base = ["How to reset password", "How
to track order", "How to return items"]

    def understand_query(self, query):
        return query.lower()

    def search_knowledge_base(self, query):
        for item in self.knowledge_base:
            if query in item.lower():
                return item
        return None

    def respond_to_query(self, query):
        understood_query = self.understand_query(query)
        response =
self.search_knowledge_base(understood_query)

        if response:
            print(f"Agent Response: {response}")
        else:
```

```
          print("Agent Response: I'm sorry, I could not
find the answer. Escalating to a human.")

# Create an agent instance
agent = CustomerSupportAgent()

# Test the agent
agent.respond_to_query("How to reset password?")
agent.respond_to_query("How to cancel order?")
```

Explanation of the Code:

- The `CustomerSupportAgent` class has a simple `knowledge_base` list containing FAQs.
- The `understand_query` method processes the query (in this case, converts it to lowercase).
- The `search_knowledge_base` method searches for the query in the knowledge base.
- The `respond_to_query` method makes decisions using **conditional logic**: if the query matches an item in the knowledge base, it provides a response; otherwise, it escalates the query.

Example Output:

```
Agent Response: How to reset password
Agent Response: I'm sorry, I could not find the answer.
Escalating to a human.
```

This basic example demonstrates how to use conditional logic to make decisions and guide the agent through its workflow.

3.3 Managing Agent States

An AI agent often has to keep track of different **states** throughout its operation. These states represent various stages in the agent's lifecycle or task completion process.

State Management Techniques

There are several ways to manage agent states:

1. **Finite State Machines (FSM):** An FSM defines a set of states and the transitions between them. Agents can only be in one state at a time and transition from one state to another based on certain conditions.
2. **State Variables:** Use variables to track the agent's current state and update it as needed.
3. **State Transitions:** A state transition occurs when the agent moves from one state to another after completing a task or meeting certain conditions.

Example: Simple State Management in a Customer Support Agent

```python
class CustomerSupportAgent:
    def __init__(self):
        self.state = "idle"
        self.knowledge_base = ["How to reset password", "How
to track order"]

    def understand_query(self, query):
        return query.lower()

    def search_knowledge_base(self, query):
        for item in self.knowledge_base:
            if query in item.lower():
                return item
        return None

    def respond_to_query(self, query):
        if self.state == "idle":
            print("Agent is ready to assist.")
            self.state = "processing"
            understood_query = self.understand_query(query)
            response =
self.search_knowledge_base(understood_query)

            if response:
                print(f"Agent Response: {response}")
            else:
                print("Agent Response: Escalating to a
human.")
            self.state = "idle"  # Returning to idle state
after processing

# Create an agent instance
agent = CustomerSupportAgent()

# Test the agent with state management
agent.respond_to_query("How to reset password?")
```

Explanation of the Code:

- The agent has a `state` variable to track whether it is idle, processing, or engaged in another task.
- Before processing a query, the agent checks if it is in the "idle" state. Once the query is processed, the agent transitions back to the "idle" state.

Example Output:

```
Agent is ready to assist.
Agent Response: How to reset password
```

Persisting Agent Data

In many applications, agents need to store and retrieve information over time. For example, an agent may need to save user interactions or task progress.

One common approach for persisting agent data is by using a **database** or **local storage** (e.g., JSON, CSV files).

Example: Saving Agent State to a File (using JSON)

```python
import json

class CustomerSupportAgent:
    def __init__(self, name):
        self.name = name
        self.state = "idle"
        self.history = []

    def save_state(self):
        with open(f"{self.name}_state.json", "w") as f:
            json.dump({"state": self.state, "history": self.history}, f)

    def load_state(self):
        try:
            with open(f"{self.name}_state.json", "r") as f:
                data = json.load(f)
                self.state = data["state"]
                self.history = data["history"]
        except FileNotFoundError:
            print(f"No previous state found for {self.name}.")
```

```python
    def log_interaction(self, query):
        self.history.append(query)
        self.save_state()

    def respond_to_query(self, query):
        self.load_state()
        if self.state == "idle":
            print("Agent is ready to assist.")
            self.state = "processing"
            self.log_interaction(query)
            print(f"Agent Response: Thank you for your query: {query}")
            self.state = "idle"
            self.save_state()

# Create an agent instance
agent = CustomerSupportAgent(name="TaskMaster")

# Simulate some queries
agent.respond_to_query("How to reset password?")
agent.respond_to_query("How to track order?")
```

Explanation of the Code:

- The `save_state` method stores the current state and interaction history to a JSON file.
- The `load_state` method loads the saved state and history when the agent starts.
- This enables the agent to persist information even when the system restarts.

3.4 Debugging and Testing Your Agents

As with any software system, debugging and testing are critical to ensure that your agent behaves as expected. Below, we'll cover common issues, solutions, and testing tools.

Common Issues and Solutions

1. **Issue: Agent Not Responding**
   - **Solution:** Check if the agent's `state` is correctly set to "idle" or "processing". Ensure there are no conditions blocking the decision-making process.

2. **Issue: Query Not Recognized**
   - o **Solution:** Verify that the `understand_query` method is correctly processing the input (e.g., handling lowercase, removing special characters).
3. **Issue: State Transitions Not Happening**
   - o **Solution:** Ensure that transitions between states (idle, processing, etc.) are properly managed, and check if the conditions for transitions are met.

Testing Frameworks and Tools

1. **Unit Testing with pytest**:
   - o Use `pytest` to write unit tests for your agents. This allows you to test individual functions like `respond_to_query` or `search_knowledge_base`.

   Example test for `CustomerSupportAgent`:

   ```
   import pytest

   def test_respond_to_query():
       agent = CustomerSupportAgent(name="TestAgent")
       agent.respond_to_query("How to reset password?")
       assert "How to reset password" in agent.history
       assert agent.state == "idle"
   ```

   - o **Run tests** with:
   - o `pytest test_agent.py`
2. **Mocking External APIs**:
   - o If your agent interacts with external APIs, use mocking to simulate API responses and test the agent's behavior without actually hitting the live API.

   Example using `unittest.mock`:

   ```
   from unittest.mock import patch

   @patch('requests.get')
   def test_external_query(mock_get):
       mock_get.return_value.status_code = 200
       agent = CustomerSupportAgent(name="TestAgent")
       agent.respond_to_query("How to track order?")
       assert mock_get.called
   ```

Summary

In this chapter, we covered:

- **Designing agent workflows**: Defining clear objectives, using flowcharts to visualize tasks.
- **Implementing simple decision-making**: Using conditional logic to make decisions and guide agents through tasks.
- **Managing agent states**: Tracking the agent's state during operation and persisting data using files.
- **Debugging and testing**: Addressing common issues and using frameworks like `pytest` for testing agent functionality.

With these foundational skills, you are now ready to build more sophisticated agents, incorporating learning algorithms and complex decision-making processes. The next chapter will dive deeper into advanced agent behaviors and machine learning integrations!

Chapter 4: Advanced Agent Behaviors

In this chapter, we will explore how to build more sophisticated AI agents by introducing **complex decision-making algorithms**, integrating **machine learning models**, leveraging **natural language processing (NLP)**, and handling **asynchronous tasks**. By the end of this chapter, you will have the tools to create agents capable of making complex decisions, interacting with users more naturally, and handling concurrent tasks efficiently.

4.1 Implementing Complex Decision-Making Algorithms

As AI agents become more advanced, their decision-making capabilities need to evolve from simple `if-else` conditions to more complex strategies. In this section, we'll discuss how to implement decision trees and graphs to enable more nuanced decision-making.

Decision Trees and Graphs

A **decision tree** is a flowchart-like structure where each internal node represents a decision based on a feature, each branch represents an outcome of that decision, and each leaf node represents a final decision or action.

Advantages of Decision Trees:

- **Interpretability:** Decision trees are easy to understand and visualize, making them ideal for transparent decision-making.
- **Non-linear Decision Making:** They can handle non-linear relationships between features.

Example of a Decision Tree: For a customer support agent, a decision tree can help decide the response based on the type of query:

1. **Is the query about account?**
    - o Yes → Ask for account verification.
    - o No → Proceed to check if it's a product-related query.
2. **Is the query about product details?**
    - o Yes → Provide product info.

o No → Escalate to human support.

Code Example:

```
class DecisionTreeAgent:
    def __init__(self):
        self.tree = {
            "account": self.handle_account_query,
            "product": self.handle_product_query,
            "default": self.escalate_to_human
        }

    def make_decision(self, query):
        if "account" in query.lower():
            return self.tree["account"](query)
        elif "product" in query.lower():
            return self.tree["product"](query)
        else:
            return self.tree["default"]()

    def handle_account_query(self, query):
        return "Please verify your account details."

    def handle_product_query(self, query):
        return "Here's the product information you
requested."

    def escalate_to_human(self):
        return "I'm escalating this to a human
representative."

# Test the decision tree agent
agent = DecisionTreeAgent()
print(agent.make_decision("I need help with my account"))
print(agent.make_decision("Tell me about your products"))
print(agent.make_decision("I want to cancel my order"))
```

Explanation:

- The agent uses a **decision tree** to classify incoming queries based on keywords ("account" and "product").
- It then calls the appropriate function to handle the query.

42

Example: Dynamic Resource Allocation Agent

Consider an AI agent responsible for managing resources (e.g., CPU, memory) in a cloud computing environment. This agent can dynamically allocate resources based on the current load.

Decision Tree for Resource Allocation:

1. **Is the CPU load high?**
    - Yes → Increase CPU allocation.
    - No → Check memory load.
2. **Is memory usage high?**
    - Yes → Increase memory allocation.
    - No → Maintain current resource allocation.

Code Example for Resource Allocation:

```python
class ResourceAllocationAgent:
    def __init__(self):
        self.cpu_usage = 40  # in percentage
        self.memory_usage = 50  # in percentage

    def allocate_resources(self):
        if self.cpu_usage > 70:
            return self.allocate_cpu()
        elif self.memory_usage > 70:
            return self.allocate_memory()
        else:
            return "Resources are optimally allocated."

    def allocate_cpu(self):
        return "Allocating more CPU resources."

    def allocate_memory(self):
        return "Allocating more memory resources."

# Test the resource allocation agent
agent = ResourceAllocationAgent()
agent.cpu_usage = 80
agent.memory_usage = 50
print(agent.allocate_resources())

agent.cpu_usage = 50
agent.memory_usage = 80
print(agent.allocate_resources())
```

Explanation:

- The agent uses a **decision tree** to determine which resource (CPU or memory) to allocate based on current usage.
- It dynamically adjusts resource allocation based on system load.

4.2 Integrating Machine Learning Models

Machine learning (ML) can significantly enhance the decision-making capabilities of AI agents by allowing them to learn from past data. By integrating ML models, agents can improve their performance over time, adapt to new conditions, and make predictions based on historical data.

Incorporating ML for Enhanced Decision Making

You can integrate ML models into your AI agent to enhance its decision-making ability. For example, a predictive maintenance agent can use historical data to predict when a machine will fail, allowing it to take proactive measures.

Steps for Integrating ML:

1. **Collect Data:** Gather historical data relevant to the agent's tasks (e.g., customer support interactions, machine performance data).
2. **Train a Model:** Use a machine learning algorithm (e.g., linear regression, decision trees) to train a model based on the collected data.
3. **Integrate the Model into the Agent:** Embed the trained model into the agent, so it can make decisions or predictions based on new input.

Example: Predictive Maintenance Agent

This agent predicts when equipment (e.g., a pump) will require maintenance based on past performance data.

Training a Simple ML Model:

```
import numpy as np
from sklearn.linear_model import LinearRegression

# Sample data: [hours of operation, temperature] -> [failure
probability]
```

```
X = np.array([[100, 30], [200, 50], [300, 70], [400, 90],
[500, 110]])  # Features
y = np.array([0, 0, 1, 1, 1])  # Labels: 0 for no failure, 1
for failure

# Train a model
model = LinearRegression()
model.fit(X, y)

# Predicting failure probability based on new data
new_data = np.array([[450, 100]])  # New data: 450 hours of
operation, 100°C
predicted_failure = model.predict(new_data)

print("Predicted failure probability:", predicted_failure[0])
```

Explanation:

- **Training Data (x)**: The agent is trained with features such as operation hours and temperature.
- **Labels (y)**: Labels represent whether the equipment failed or not.
- **Prediction**: The agent predicts the likelihood of failure based on the input data.

Output:

```
Predicted failure probability: 0.99
```

4.3 Natural Language Processing (NLP) in Agents

Natural Language Processing (NLP) allows agents to interact with humans in a more natural way by understanding and processing human language. NLP is critical for developing chatbots, virtual assistants, and customer service agents.

Leveraging NLP for Better Interactions

NLP enables agents to:

- **Understand user intent**: Determine the meaning behind the user's words.
- **Generate human-like responses**: Provide responses that sound natural and contextually relevant.

- **Handle ambiguous inputs**: Deal with uncertainty in language and ask clarifying questions if needed.

Example: Intelligent Chatbot Agent

Let's create a simple chatbot agent that can understand and respond to user queries. We'll use the `nltk` library for basic NLP tasks like tokenization and keyword matching.

Code Example:

```python
import nltk
from nltk.tokenize import word_tokenize

class ChatbotAgent:
    def __init__(self):
        self.responses = {
            "hello": "Hi! How can I help you today?",
            "bye": "Goodbye! Have a great day!",
            "default": "Sorry, I didn't understand that."
        }

    def process_query(self, query):
        tokens = word_tokenize(query.lower())
        for word in tokens:
            if word in self.responses:
                return self.responses[word]
        return self.responses["default"]

# Create a chatbot instance
chatbot = ChatbotAgent()

# Test the chatbot
print(chatbot.process_query("Hello!"))
print(chatbot.process_query("Can you help me?"))
print(chatbot.process_query("Bye"))
```

Explanation:

- The agent tokenizes the user's query and checks if any tokens match predefined keywords.
- If it finds a match (e.g., "hello" or "bye"), it provides the corresponding response; otherwise, it returns a default message.

Example Output:

```
Hi! How can I help you today?
Sorry, I didn't understand that.
Goodbye! Have a great day!
```

4.4 Handling Asynchronous Tasks

Asynchronous tasks are essential for building responsive and efficient agents, especially in environments where real-time data processing is required (e.g., live customer interactions, streaming data).

Managing Concurrent Processes

Managing concurrent processes allows agents to perform multiple tasks simultaneously, rather than waiting for one task to finish before starting another. In Python, the `asyncio` library is commonly used to handle asynchronous programming.

Example: Real-Time Data Processing Agent

Let's create an agent that can process multiple data streams concurrently, simulating a real-time monitoring system for environmental sensors.

Code Example:

```python
import asyncio

class RealTimeAgent:
    def __init__(self):
        self.data_streams = ["temperature", "humidity",
"pressure"]

    async def process_data(self, stream):
        print(f"Processing {stream} data...")
        await asyncio.sleep(2)  # Simulate data processing
        print(f"Finished processing {stream} data.")

    async def run(self):
        tasks = [self.process_data(stream) for stream in
self.data_streams]
        await asyncio.gather(*tasks)

# Create a real-time agent instance
agent = RealTimeAgent()

# Run the agent to process all data streams concurrently
```

```
asyncio.run(agent.run())
```

Explanation:

- The `process_data` method simulates processing a data stream with a delay of 2 seconds.
- The `run` method gathers all the tasks and processes them concurrently using `asyncio.gather`.

Example Output:

```
Processing temperature data...
Processing humidity data...
Processing pressure data...
Finished processing temperature data.
Finished processing humidity data.
Finished processing pressure data.
```

Summary

In this chapter, we covered:

- **Implementing complex decision-making algorithms**: Using decision trees to manage agent behaviors and resource allocation.
- **Integrating machine learning models**: How to incorporate ML models to enhance agent decision-making capabilities, with a focus on predictive maintenance.
- **Leveraging NLP**: Using natural language processing to improve human-agent interactions, including a simple chatbot example.
- **Handling asynchronous tasks**: Using `asyncio` to process multiple tasks concurrently, making the agent responsive in real-time environments.

These advanced agent behaviors set the foundation for creating more intelligent and adaptable AI systems capable of tackling complex real-world tasks. In the next chapter, we will explore how to manage agent states effectively and persist agent data to improve long-term performance.

Chapter 5: Multi-Agent Systems

In this chapter, we will explore the concept of **multi-agent systems (MAS)** and how they enable multiple AI agents to work together to achieve common or individual goals. We'll discuss multi-agent architectures, coordination strategies, conflict resolution mechanisms, and the scalability of such systems. By the end of this chapter, you will understand how to build and manage a system composed of multiple interacting agents, enabling them to solve complex problems in a collaborative environment.

5.1 Introduction to Multi-Agent Architectures

Benefits and Challenges

Multi-agent systems (MAS) consist of multiple AI agents that can collaborate, compete, or independently pursue goals within a shared environment. These systems are used in a wide range of applications, such as robotics, traffic management, supply chains, and financial trading. Let's first explore the key **benefits** and **challenges** of using multi-agent architectures.

Benefits:

1. **Task Decomposition**:
    -   Complex problems can be broken down into smaller tasks, which individual agents can solve independently, leading to more efficient problem-solving.
    -   For example, in a **robotics system**, one agent may be responsible for navigation while another handles object recognition.
2. **Parallelism and Efficiency**:
    -   Multiple agents working concurrently can significantly reduce the time required to complete tasks.
    -   **Example**: In a **manufacturing system**, different agents can handle different parts of the production process simultaneously, speeding up the overall operation.
3. **Flexibility and Scalability**:
    -   Multi-agent systems are inherently flexible, allowing for easy addition or removal of agents based on the system's needs.

- o For instance, a **smart city system** might scale by adding more traffic management agents as the city grows.
4. **Robustness**:
   - o A failure in one agent does not lead to the failure of the entire system. Other agents can continue functioning, ensuring the system remains operational.
   - o This is crucial in systems like **healthcare**, where different agents might handle different aspects of patient care, ensuring continuity despite individual failures.

Challenges:

1. **Coordination and Collaboration**:
   - o Ensuring agents coordinate their actions efficiently can be difficult, especially when agents are working towards different goals or objectives.
   - o Poor coordination can lead to inefficient solutions or even conflict between agents.
2. **Communication Overhead**:
   - o In MAS, agents need to communicate with each other to share information. This can lead to communication overhead, which can slow down the system if not managed properly.
   - o For example, agents in a **multi-agent robot system** need to share sensor data and states, and excessive communication can delay decision-making.
3. **Conflict Resolution**:
   - o In MAS, agents may have conflicting goals or interests. Ensuring that agents can resolve conflicts without disrupting the system is critical.
   - o For instance, in a **financial trading system**, agents may compete for limited resources or trading opportunities.
4. **Distributed Control**:
   - o In MAS, there is no single point of control, making it challenging to monitor and manage the system as a whole.
   - o This requires careful design of communication protocols and decision-making strategies to ensure effective control over the system.

Communication Protocols

Communication is the backbone of multi-agent systems. Agents must be able to share information and coordinate their actions effectively. There are various communication protocols used in MAS, including:

1. **Message Passing**:
   - Agents communicate by sending messages to each other. Each message typically contains information about the agent's state, actions, or requests.
   - **Example Protocol**: The **KQML** (Knowledge Query and Manipulation Language) protocol allows agents to send messages about actions, goals, and requests.
2. **Blackboard Systems**:
   - A central "blackboard" is shared by all agents, and each agent can read from and write to the blackboard. This is useful in collaborative tasks where multiple agents contribute to solving a problem.
   - **Example**: In a **medical diagnosis system**, different agents (like symptom checkers, diagnosis engines) contribute their knowledge to a shared blackboard to arrive at a conclusion.
3. **Agent Communication Languages (ACLs)**:
   - These are formal languages designed for agent communication. The **FIPA-ACL** (Foundation for Intelligent Physical Agents – Agent Communication Language) is widely used for multi-agent communication.
   - FIPA-ACL includes specific speech acts (e.g., **request**, **inform**, **subscribe**) that agents can use to interact.
4. **Shared Memory**:
   - Agents share a common memory space to exchange information. This is typically used when agents are co-located or in close proximity to each other.
   - For example, in a **robot swarm**, agents can share information about the environment through a shared memory space, allowing them to collaborate in real-time.

5.2 Coordination and Collaboration Between Agents

Effective coordination is essential for the success of any multi-agent system. Agents must work together to complete tasks, share resources, and avoid duplication of efforts. In this section, we'll discuss **coordination strategies** and how collaboration can be managed between agents.

Coordination Strategies

1. **Centralized Coordination**:
   o A central controller or coordinator oversees the actions of all agents. The coordinator makes decisions on behalf of the agents, ensuring that they work together efficiently.
   o **Example**: In a **warehouse management system**, a central system coordinates robot agents to pick, pack, and move items based on a schedule.
2. **Decentralized Coordination**:
   o In decentralized systems, agents make their own decisions and coordinate without a central authority. This method is more flexible and scalable, but it can lead to inefficiencies if coordination is not properly handled.
   o **Example**: In **autonomous vehicle fleets**, each vehicle makes its own decisions regarding navigation, but they must coordinate with other vehicles to avoid collisions.
3. **Cooperative Coordination**:
   o Agents work together, each contributing to the success of the group. This often involves sharing resources, information, or tasks to achieve a common goal.
   o **Example**: In **disaster response scenarios**, multiple agents (such as drones, search-and-rescue robots) cooperate to search for survivors and deliver supplies.
4. **Competitive Coordination**:
   o Agents may have competing goals, such as maximizing their own utility. This type of coordination requires mechanisms to ensure fairness and prevent conflicts.
   o **Example**: In **auctions or financial markets**, agents (traders) compete for limited resources (e.g., stocks or assets), and coordination mechanisms ensure fairness and optimal outcomes.

Example: Collaborative Supply Chain Agents

In a **supply chain management system**, multiple agents can be used to handle different aspects, such as inventory management, order fulfillment, and shipping. These agents need to coordinate their actions to ensure smooth operations.

Code Example:

```python
class SupplyChainAgent:
    def __init__(self, name):
        self.name = name
        self.inventory = 100  # initial inventory

    def check_inventory(self):
        return self.inventory

    def order_inventory(self, amount):
        self.inventory += amount
        print(f"{self.name} ordered {amount} units of
inventory.")

    def fulfill_order(self, amount):
        if self.inventory >= amount:
            self.inventory -= amount
            print(f"{self.name} fulfilled an order of
{amount} units.")
        else:
            print(f"{self.name} cannot fulfill order.
Insufficient inventory.")

# Create supply chain agents
supplier = SupplyChainAgent(name="Supplier 1")
retailer = SupplyChainAgent(name="Retailer 1")

# Order inventory and fulfill orders
supplier.order_inventory(50)
retailer.fulfill_order(30)
```

Explanation:

- Each agent (supplier and retailer) has its own inventory and must work together to fulfill orders.
- The supplier orders more inventory, and the retailer fulfills customer orders based on available stock.
- Coordination between agents ensures that both parties operate efficiently within the supply chain.

5.3 Conflict Resolution Mechanisms

In a multi-agent system, agents may have conflicting goals, such as competing for resources, tasks, or information. It is important to design effective **conflict resolution mechanisms** to ensure smooth operations.

Detecting and Resolving Conflicts

1. **Conflict Detection**:
   - Conflicts can arise when two or more agents try to access the same resource, perform the same task, or make contradictory decisions.
   - **Example**: In **multi-agent robotic systems**, agents may try to access the same workspace or tool at the same time.
2. **Conflict Resolution Techniques**:
   - **Negotiation**: Agents negotiate to reach a mutually acceptable solution. This is common when agents have competing goals but can find common ground through communication.
   - **Mediation**: A neutral agent (mediator) helps resolve disputes between conflicting agents by proposing a compromise.
   - **Priority-based Systems**: Assign priority levels to agents, so higher-priority agents are allowed to execute their tasks first.
   - **Task Redistribution**: If conflicts arise due to resource allocation, tasks can be reassigned to different agents to balance the load.

Example: Traffic Management Agents

In a **traffic management system**, multiple agents control traffic lights, pedestrian signals, and flow direction. Conflicts may arise if two traffic light agents attempt to change the light on the same intersection simultaneously.

Code Example:

```python
class TrafficAgent:
    def __init__(self, name, location):
        self.name = name
        self.location = location
        self.light_status = "red"

    def change_light(self, status):
        if self.light_status != status:
            self.light_status = status
```

```python
            print(f"{self.name} changed light to
{self.light_status} at {self.location}.")
        else:
            print(f"{self.name}: No change in light status at
{self.location}.")

# Create traffic agents at different locations
agent1 = TrafficAgent(name="Agent 1", location="Intersection
A")
agent2 = TrafficAgent(name="Agent 2", location="Intersection
B")

# Resolving conflict with priority-based system
if agent1.light_status == "green":
    agent1.change_light("red")
else:
    agent2.change_light("green")
```

Explanation:

- Two traffic agents are in conflict over the control of lights at different intersections. The priority-based system resolves the conflict by allowing one agent to control the light based on its current state.

5.4 Scaling Multi-Agent Systems

As multi-agent systems grow, scalability becomes crucial. In large systems, the number of agents may increase, and the system needs to handle more complex tasks and interactions without performance degradation.

Techniques for Scalability

1. **Distributed Systems**:
   o In a distributed MAS, agents are spread across multiple machines or nodes, reducing the load on any single machine and enabling better performance as the system scales.
   o **Example**: In a **distributed sensor network**, sensors (agents) are deployed in various locations, each collecting data and working independently.
2. **Load Balancing**:
   o Load balancing techniques distribute tasks across multiple agents to prevent any one agent from becoming overwhelmed.

- o **Example**: In a **cloud-based system**, multiple agents can handle different regions or types of requests to balance processing power.
3. **Hierarchical Structures**:
   - o Use hierarchical coordination, where higher-level agents manage lower-level agents, making it easier to manage large numbers of agents.
   - o **Example**: In a **robotic assembly line**, managers coordinate several teams of robots to streamline production.
4. **Event-Driven Architecture**:
   - o Agents respond to events rather than polling or continuously checking for changes, which reduces unnecessary processing and allows the system to scale more efficiently.
   - o **Example**: In a **smart home system**, devices (agents) only perform actions when specific triggers or events occur.

Performance Optimization

1. **Caching and Data Aggregation**:
   - o Caching commonly requested data can improve performance by reducing the need to recompute or retrieve data from distant agents.
   - o **Example**: A **content delivery network (CDN)** uses caching to quickly serve content to users without requesting it from the origin server.
2. **Efficient Communication**:
   - o Optimize communication between agents to reduce overhead. This can include using more efficient message formats or compressing data before transmission.
   - o **Example**: In a **multi-agent system for supply chain management**, agents can periodically synchronize their states rather than continuously sending updates.
3. **Parallel Processing**:
   - o Utilize parallel processing to speed up computations and tasks, especially for data-heavy systems.
   - o **Example**: In a **multi-agent financial trading system**, multiple agents can process and analyze different market conditions in parallel.

Summary

In this chapter, we explored:

- **Multi-agent architectures**: We discussed the benefits and challenges of using MAS, as well as key communication protocols like message passing and shared memory.
- **Coordination strategies**: We examined how agents can collaborate and coordinate through centralized, decentralized, and competitive models.
- **Conflict resolution**: We learned methods for detecting and resolving conflicts between agents, ensuring smooth system operation.
- **Scalability**: We discussed techniques for scaling MAS, including distributed systems, load balancing, and hierarchical structures, as well as performance optimization strategies.

With these concepts, you can design and manage systems composed of multiple agents that work together to solve complex problems. In the next chapter, we will focus on managing agent states and persistence, ensuring that agents retain their information and maintain context over time.

Chapter 6: Reinforcement Learning for AI Agents

In this chapter, we will dive deep into **Reinforcement Learning (RL)**, a powerful machine learning technique that enables agents to learn how to perform tasks through trial and error. RL is widely used in autonomous systems, robotics, gaming, and decision-making scenarios. We will cover the fundamentals of RL, how to implement RL in LangGraph agents, training and evaluation strategies, and advanced RL techniques such as **Deep Reinforcement Learning** and **Multi-Agent RL**. By the end of this chapter, you will have a solid understanding of how to build and train intelligent agents using RL.

6.1 Fundamentals of Reinforcement Learning (RL)

Key Concepts and Terminology

At the heart of **Reinforcement Learning** is the concept of an agent that interacts with an environment and learns from feedback. The key concepts and terminology in RL include:

1. **Agent**:
   - The entity that makes decisions and takes actions in an environment. In our case, this is typically an AI agent, like a robot or a chatbot.
2. **Environment**:
   - The external system or world with which the agent interacts. The environment provides feedback (rewards or penalties) based on the agent's actions.
3. **State (s)**:
   - The current condition or situation of the environment. A state represents all the information needed for the agent to make a decision.
4. **Action (a)**:
   - The decisions or moves an agent can make. Actions are taken by the agent to interact with the environment.
5. **Reward (r)**:

- The feedback given by the environment after an action is taken. Rewards can be positive (reinforcing a behavior) or negative (punishing undesirable behavior).

6. **Policy (π)**:
   - A strategy or mapping from states to actions. The policy defines the agent's behavior at any given state, guiding it on what action to take.

7. **Value Function (V(s))**:
   - A function that estimates the expected future reward an agent can get from a state. It helps the agent evaluate which states are more valuable.

8. **Q-Function (Q(s, a))**:
   - The Q-value represents the expected future reward of taking action aa in state ss and following a given policy thereafter. The Q-function is a central concept in RL algorithms like Q-learning.

9. **Episode**:
   - A sequence of interactions between the agent and the environment, ending in a terminal state or a goal being achieved. For example, in a game, an episode may end when a player wins or loses.

10. **Discount Factor (γ)**:
    - A factor that represents the importance of future rewards compared to immediate rewards. A high value of γ encourages the agent to focus on long-term rewards, while a low value favors short-term gains.

RL Algorithms Overview

There are several RL algorithms, each suited for different types of problems. Here's an overview of some of the most popular RL algorithms:

1. **Q-Learning**:
   - A model-free RL algorithm that learns the optimal action-value function (Q-function). The agent uses Q-values to determine the best action to take for a given state.

   Q-Learning Algorithm:

   - Update rule:

$$Q(s,a) \leftarrow Q(s,a) + \alpha[r + \gamma \max a' Q(s',a') - Q(s,a)] Q(s, a) \leftarrow Q(s, a) + \alpha \left[r + \gamma \max\_{a'} Q(s', a') - Q(s, a) \right]$$

where:

- α \alpha is the learning rate.
- r r is the immediate reward.
- γ \gamma is the discount factor.
- s' s' is the next state.
- a' a' is the next action.

2. **SARSA (State-Action-Reward-State-Action)**:
   - A model-free algorithm similar to Q-learning but differs in how the future reward is calculated. SARSA updates the Q-value based on the action taken by the agent in the next state, rather than the best possible action.

3. **Deep Q-Networks (DQN)**:
   - A deep learning extension of Q-learning. Instead of using a table to store Q-values, DQN uses a neural network to approximate the Q-function, enabling it to handle larger, more complex environments.

4. **Policy Gradient Methods**:
   - These methods focus on directly optimizing the policy without estimating value functions. They are particularly useful for environments with high-dimensional action spaces.
   - **REINFORCE** is a popular policy gradient algorithm.

5. **Actor-Critic Methods**:
   - These algorithms combine both value-based and policy-based methods. The **actor** updates the policy, while the **critic** evaluates the policy using a value function.

6.2 Implementing RL in LangGraph Agents

Now that we understand the basic concepts of RL, let's explore how to implement it in **LangGraph**. We'll start by setting up RL environments and implementing a simple RL agent that can perform tasks like autonomous navigation.

Setting Up RL Environments

An **RL environment** is an interface that the agent interacts with. In LangGraph, environments can be designed using Python libraries such as **OpenAI Gym**, which provides a variety of pre-built environments for training RL agents.

Installing OpenAI Gym:

```
pip install gym
```

Once you have Gym installed, you can create your RL environment. Let's consider a basic environment where an agent needs to navigate a simple grid.

```python
import gym

# Create a simple environment (e.g., CartPole, a basic
reinforcement learning environment)
env = gym.make('CartPole-v1')  # 'CartPole-v1' is a common
test environment

# Initialize the environment
state = env.reset()

# Running a basic loop where the agent takes random actions
for _ in range(1000):
    env.render()  # Display the environment
    action = env.action_space.sample()  # Randomly choose an
action
    state, reward, done, info = env.step(action)  # Take
action and get feedback

    if done:
        state = env.reset()  # Reset the environment if the
episode is done

env.close()  # Close the environment after the simulation
```

Explanation:

- **Gym Environment**: We use **OpenAI Gym** to simulate a **CartPole** environment, where an agent must balance a pole on a moving cart.
- **Rendering**: The render() method displays the current state of the environment.

- **Random Actions**: The agent takes random actions (using `sample()`), and the environment responds by returning the next state, reward, and a flag indicating whether the episode is finished.
- **Loop**: The agent continues taking actions until the episode ends and then resets the environment.

Example: Autonomous Navigation Agent

Let's implement a **simple autonomous navigation agent** that can navigate through a grid world environment using Q-learning.

Code Example:

```python
import numpy as np
import random

class GridWorldEnv:
    def __init__(self, grid_size=(5, 5), goal=(4, 4)):
        self.grid_size = grid_size
        self.goal = goal
        self.state = (0, 0)  # Start position at the top-left
corner

    def reset(self):
        self.state = (0, 0)  # Reset state to the starting
position
        return self.state

    def step(self, action):
        x, y = self.state
        if action == 0:  # Move Up
            x = max(0, x - 1)
        elif action == 1:  # Move Right
            y = min(self.grid_size[1] - 1, y + 1)
        elif action == 2:  # Move Down
            x = min(self.grid_size[0] - 1, x + 1)
        elif action == 3:  # Move Left
            y = max(0, y - 1)

        self.state = (x, y)
        reward = -1
        if self.state == self.goal:
            reward = 10  # Reward for reaching the goal
        return self.state, reward, self.state == self.goal

class QLearningAgent:
```

```python
    def __init__(self, env):
        self.env = env
        self.q_table = np.zeros((env.grid_size[0],
env.grid_size[1], 4))  # Q-table: States x Actions
        self.learning_rate = 0.1
        self.discount_factor = 0.9
        self.exploration_rate = 1.0  # Start with 100%
exploration
        self.exploration_decay = 0.995

    def choose_action(self, state):
        if random.uniform(0, 1) < self.exploration_rate:
            return random.randint(0, 3)  # Random action
(exploration)
        else:
            return np.argmax(self.q_table[state[0],
state[1]])  # Best action (exploitation)

    def update_q_table(self, state, action, reward,
next_state):
        best_next_action =
np.argmax(self.q_table[next_state[0], next_state[1]])
        current_q_value = self.q_table[state[0], state[1],
action]
        future_q_value = self.q_table[next_state[0],
next_state[1], best_next_action]
        new_q_value = current_q_value + self.learning_rate *
(reward + self.discount_factor * future_q_value -
current_q_value)
        self.q_table[state[0], state[1], action] =
new_q_value

    def train(self, episodes=1000):
        for episode in range(episodes):
            state = self.env.reset()
            done = False
            while not done:
                action = self.choose_action(state)
                next_state, reward, done =
self.env.step(action)
                self.update_q_table(state, action, reward,
next_state)
                state = next_state
            self.exploration_rate *= self.exploration_decay
# Decay exploration rate

# Train the Q-learning agent
env = GridWorldEnv()
agent = QLearningAgent(env)
agent.train(episodes=500)
```

```
# After training, let's see the learned policy
print("Learned Q-table:")
print(agent.q_table)
```

Explanation:

- **GridWorldEnv**: This is a simple environment where an agent moves within a grid. The agent's goal is to reach the bottom-right corner of the grid (goal position `(4,4)`).
- **QLearningAgent**: This agent uses **Q-learning** to learn the optimal action policy. It updates the Q-values based on the feedback it receives after each action.
- **Training**: The agent explores the environment, updates the Q-values, and gradually learns the best actions to take in each state to maximize the reward.

Learning Process: During training, the agent explores the grid, learns from each step, and improves its Q-values. Over time, it reduces exploration and focuses more on exploiting its learned policy.

6.3 Training and Evaluating RL Models

Training RL models is a dynamic process where an agent learns to make better decisions over time through interactions with its environment.

Training Strategies

1. **Exploration vs. Exploitation**:
   o In RL, there's a trade-off between exploration (trying new actions) and exploitation (choosing the best-known action). A balance is essential for learning efficiently.
   o During training, the agent starts by exploring many actions (high exploration) and gradually shifts towards exploitation as it learns the optimal policy.
2. **Learning Rate (α)**:
   o The learning rate determines how quickly the agent updates its Q-values based on new information. A high learning rate allows for rapid adaptation but may lead to instability, while a low learning rate ensures stable learning but may slow down the process.

3. **Discount Factor (γ)**:
   - o The discount factor controls the importance of future rewards. A high discount factor encourages the agent to focus on long-term rewards, while a low discount factor favors immediate rewards.
4. **Batch vs. Online Learning**:
   - o **Batch Learning** involves training the agent on a batch of experiences collected over time.
   - o **Online Learning** updates the model after each interaction, making it more adaptive to immediate changes in the environment.

Performance Metrics

1. **Total Reward**:
   - o The total accumulated reward over an episode is a basic metric for evaluating an agent's performance. Higher total rewards generally indicate better performance.
2. **Convergence**:
   - o Convergence refers to the point where the agent's policy stabilizes, meaning it consistently makes the same decisions for the same states. Convergence is often measured by the change in the Q-table or policy over time.
3. **Success Rate**:
   - o This metric measures how often the agent achieves its goal within a given number of steps or episodes. It's particularly useful for tasks where the agent must complete specific objectives.

6.4 Advanced RL Techniques

Deep Reinforcement Learning

Deep Reinforcement Learning (DRL) combines deep learning with RL to handle environments with high-dimensional state and action spaces. Traditional RL methods like Q-learning struggle with large state spaces (e.g., images, videos), but DRL uses deep neural networks to approximate the Q-values or policies.

Deep Q-Network (DQN) is a popular DRL algorithm where a neural network is used to approximate the Q-value function.

Code Example:

```
import torch
import torch.nn as nn
import torch.optim as optim

class DQN(nn.Module):
    def __init__(self, input_size, output_size):
        super(DQN, self).__init__()
        self.fc1 = nn.Linear(input_size, 128)
        self.fc2 = nn.Linear(128, output_size)

    def forward(self, x):
        x = torch.relu(self.fc1(x))
        x = self.fc2(x)
        return x

# Example of initializing the DQN network
input_size = 4  # Example input size for CartPole environment
(state space size)
output_size = 2  # Example output size (number of actions)

dqn = DQN(input_size, output_size)
print(dqn)
```

Explanation:

- **Neural Network (DQN)**: The DQN network has two fully connected layers. The input represents the state of the environment, and the output represents the action-value for each possible action.
- **Training DQN**: The DQN model is trained using the **Bellman equation** and **Q-learning** updates, with the neural network serving as an approximator for the Q-values.

Multi-Agent RL

In **Multi-Agent RL (MARL)**, multiple agents interact with each other and the environment. They can cooperate, compete, or both, to maximize their own or collective rewards.

1. **Cooperative Multi-Agent RL**:
   o In cooperative MARL, agents work together to achieve a common goal, like in a collaborative robotics task.

2. **Competitive Multi-Agent RL**:
    - ○ In competitive MARL, agents may have opposing goals, like in a game-theory setting where agents compete for limited resources (e.g., in trading systems or adversarial games).

Example: Multi-Agent Navigation in a Grid:

- Two agents must navigate to different goals in the same grid without colliding. They need to cooperate by sharing information about their positions and avoid competing for the same space.

Summary

In this chapter, we explored:

- **Reinforcement Learning**: The key concepts of RL, including states, actions, rewards, policies, and value functions.
- **Implementing RL in LangGraph**: How to create RL environments and apply Q-learning for autonomous navigation.
- **Training and Evaluating RL Models**: Strategies for training RL agents, balancing exploration and exploitation, and evaluating agent performance.
- **Advanced RL Techniques**: Introduction to Deep Reinforcement Learning (DQN) and Multi-Agent RL, enabling agents to handle complex, high-dimensional tasks and work together or against each other.

With these advanced techniques, you can create powerful, adaptive AI agents capable of learning from their environments and improving their performance over time. In the next chapter, we will explore how to integrate RL agents into more complex systems and optimize their behavior for real-world applications.

Chapter 7: Integrating External Systems and APIs

In this chapter, we will explore how to integrate **external systems** and **APIs** into your AI agents. By connecting agents to external data sources and leveraging third-party services, you can extend the capabilities of your agents and enable them to perform more complex tasks. We'll also cover how to ensure **data security** and **privacy** when integrating with external systems, an essential consideration for maintaining trust and compliance.

7.1 Connecting to External Data Sources

AI agents can significantly benefit from connecting to external data sources. These sources can include real-time APIs, databases, and webhooks, providing agents with the information they need to make informed decisions and take appropriate actions.

APIs, Databases, and Webhooks

1. **APIs (Application Programming Interfaces)**:
   - APIs are a popular way for agents to interact with external systems. They allow agents to request data or services from another system and receive a response in a structured format, typically JSON or XML.
   - Common uses for APIs include accessing weather data, financial information, social media feeds, and much more.
2. **Databases**:
   - External databases store structured data that agents may need to access. Databases like **MySQL**, **PostgreSQL**, or **MongoDB** can hold information such as user profiles, transaction records, product inventories, etc.
   - Agents can interact with databases using SQL or NoSQL queries to retrieve or update data.
3. **Webhooks**:
   - A **webhook** is a way for one system to send real-time data to another system over HTTP. Webhooks are often used to notify an agent when an event occurs in an external system (e.g., a new payment, a new user registration).

- Webhooks are particularly useful for real-time, event-driven applications.

Example: Financial Data Integration Agent

Let's create a simple **Financial Data Integration Agent** that connects to a stock market API to retrieve the latest financial data.

Steps to Integrate Financial Data:

1. Use the **Alpha Vantage API** to get financial data for a particular stock.
2. Parse the returned data (in JSON format).
3. Provide insights based on the stock data (e.g., price trends, percentage change).

Code Example:

```python
import requests

class FinancialDataAgent:
    def __init__(self, api_key):
        self.api_key = api_key
        self.base_url = "https://www.alphavantage.co/query"

    def get_stock_data(self, symbol):
        params = {
            'function': 'TIME_SERIES_INTRADAY',
            'symbol': symbol,
            'interval': '5min',  # Interval for data (5-
minute candlesticks)
            'apikey': self.api_key
        }
        response = requests.get(self.base_url, params=params)
        data = response.json()

        if 'Time Series (5min)' in data:
            return data['Time Series (5min)']
        else:
            return "Error: No data available"

    def analyze_data(self, symbol):
        stock_data = self.get_stock_data(symbol)
        if isinstance(stock_data, dict):
            latest_data = list(stock_data.values())[0]  # Get
the latest entry
            open_price = float(latest_data['1. open'])
```

```
            close_price = float(latest_data['4. close'])
            change_percentage = ((close_price - open_price) /
open_price) * 100
            return f"The stock price for {symbol} changed by
{change_percentage:.2f}% today."
        else:
            return stock_data

# Example usage
api_key = 'YOUR_ALPHA_VANTAGE_API_KEY'  # You will need to
obtain an API key from Alpha Vantage
agent = FinancialDataAgent(api_key)
print(agent.analyze_data("AAPL"))  # Get data for Apple Inc.
```

Explanation:

- The `FinancialDataAgent` class uses the **Alpha Vantage API** to fetch real-time stock market data for a given symbol (e.g., Apple Inc. with the symbol "AAPL").
- The `analyze_data` method calculates the percentage change in the stock price between the open and close of the latest trading interval.
- **`requests.get`** sends an HTTP request to the API endpoint, and the response is parsed to retrieve the necessary stock data.

Note: You will need to obtain an API key from Alpha Vantage.

7.2 Leveraging Third-Party Services

To enhance the functionality of your agent, you can integrate third-party services. These services provide specialized functionalities that can complement the agent's capabilities, such as cloud services for processing data, or microservices for handling specific tasks.

Cloud Services and Microservices

1. **Cloud Services**:
    o **Cloud platforms** like **AWS, Google Cloud**, and **Azure** offer a wide range of services that can be integrated with your agents. These services may include computing resources, machine learning models, storage, and databases.

- o **Example**: Using **AWS Lambda** to run functions in the cloud when triggered by an event, or integrating **Google Cloud Vision** to process images.
2. **Microservices**:
   - o **Microservices** are small, independent services that perform specific tasks. Agents can communicate with these microservices to offload certain responsibilities, such as sending emails, processing payments, or managing databases.
   - o **Example**: A **payment processing microservice** could be integrated into a shopping cart agent to handle user transactions.

Example: Weather Forecasting Agent

Let's build an agent that retrieves weather data using a third-party service like the **OpenWeatherMap API**.

Code Example:

```python
import requests

class WeatherForecastAgent:
    def __init__(self, api_key):
        self.api_key = api_key
        self.base_url =
"http://api.openweathermap.org/data/2.5/weather"

    def get_weather(self, city):
        params = {
            'q': city,
            'appid': self.api_key,
            'units': 'metric'  # Temperature in Celsius
        }
        response = requests.get(self.base_url, params=params)
        data = response.json()

        if data['cod'] == 200:
            main_data = data['main']
            weather_description =
data['weather'][0]['description']
            temperature = main_data['temp']
            return f"The weather in {city} is
{weather_description} with a temperature of {temperature}°C."
        else:
            return "Error: Unable to fetch weather data"

# Example usage
```

```
api_key = 'YOUR_OPENWEATHERMAP_API_KEY'  # You will need to
obtain an API key from OpenWeatherMap
agent = WeatherForecastAgent(api_key)
print(agent.get_weather("London"))
```

Explanation:

- This agent connects to the **OpenWeatherMap API**, which provides weather information for a specific city.
- The agent sends an HTTP GET request with the city name and API key, and then processes the returned data to display the weather description and temperature.
- The response from the API is in **JSON format**, which is parsed to extract the relevant weather details.

Note: You can obtain an API key from OpenWeatherMap.

7.3 Ensuring Data Security and Privacy

When integrating external systems and APIs, data security and privacy are critical concerns. AI agents may handle sensitive information such as personal data, financial transactions, and private communications. Ensuring that this data is protected against unauthorized access and misuse is essential.

Best Practices for Secure Integrations

1. **Use Secure Communication (HTTPS)**:
   o Always use **HTTPS** for communication between your agents and external APIs to ensure that data is encrypted during transmission. Avoid using HTTP, which is unencrypted and vulnerable to attacks.
2. **API Key Management**:
   o Store API keys securely. Never hard-code them directly into your codebase or expose them in public repositories.
   o Use **environment variables** or a **secret management service** (like **AWS Secrets Manager** or **HashiCorp Vault**) to securely manage API keys and other sensitive credentials.
3. **Authentication and Authorization**:
   o When integrating with external services, ensure that proper **authentication** (e.g., using OAuth tokens or API keys) and

authorization mechanisms are in place to limit access to sensitive data.

4. **Data Encryption**:
   - Ensure that sensitive data is encrypted both at rest and in transit. Use strong encryption standards (e.g., **AES-256**) to protect data stored in databases or cloud services.

5. **Input Validation**:
   - Always validate inputs from external sources, such as API responses or user-provided data, to prevent **SQL injection**, **cross-site scripting (XSS)**, or **malicious payloads**.

Compliance Considerations

When dealing with sensitive data, compliance with regulations such as **GDPR** (General Data Protection Regulation), **CCPA** (California Consumer Privacy Act), or **HIPAA** (Health Insurance Portability and Accountability Act) is crucial. Ensure that your agent meets the following requirements:

1. **Data Minimization**:
   - Only collect the data that is necessary for the specific task. Avoid collecting unnecessary personal information.

2. **Data Storage**:
   - Ensure that any personal data is stored securely and that you follow the relevant legal guidelines for data retention and deletion.

3. **User Consent**:
   - Obtain explicit consent from users before collecting, processing, or storing their personal data. Ensure that users are informed about how their data will be used.

4. **Data Access**:
   - Implement strict access controls to ensure that only authorized personnel or systems can access sensitive data.

5. **Regular Audits**:
   - Conduct regular security audits and vulnerability assessments to ensure that your integrations remain secure over time.

Summary

In this chapter, we covered the following key topics:

- **Connecting to External Data Sources**: How to integrate external APIs, databases, and webhooks to enrich your AI agents with external information.
- **Leveraging Third-Party Services**: How to use cloud services and microservices to offload tasks and enhance agent capabilities, with examples like a weather forecasting agent.
- **Ensuring Data Security and Privacy**: Best practices for secure integrations, including the use of HTTPS, API key management, data encryption, and ensuring compliance with privacy regulations like GDPR.

By following the guidelines and examples in this chapter, you can integrate your AI agents with a wide variety of external systems, enabling them to perform more complex and useful tasks while maintaining the security and privacy of sensitive data. In the next chapter, we will explore best practices for deploying and scaling AI agents in real-world environments.

Chapter 8: Deployment and Scaling of AI Agents

In this chapter, we will explore how to deploy and scale AI agents in real-world environments. Deployment is a crucial phase in the life cycle of AI agents, as it transitions them from development to production. We will cover the essential steps involved in preparing for deployment, setting up continuous integration and deployment (CI/CD) pipelines, monitoring agent performance, scaling strategies, and emerging trends in AI deployment.

8.1 Preparing for Deployment

Before deploying your AI agents, it is essential to ensure that the environment is correctly configured and that the agents are packaged and ready to be integrated into the production environment. In this section, we'll discuss environment configuration and the process of containerization with Docker.

Environment Configuration

Proper environment configuration ensures that the agent behaves as expected when deployed. This includes configuring dependencies, managing system requirements, and setting up the correct runtime environment. Here are the essential steps for preparing the environment:

1. **Dependencies**:
   - Ensure that all required libraries and packages are installed. This can be managed using **pip** (for Python) or **npm** (for JavaScript), or any other package manager based on the language you're using.
   - Example for Python:
   - ```pip install -r requirements.txt```
   - **requirements.txt** is a file that contains all the dependencies for the project.
2. **Configuration Files**:
   - Agents may require different configuration files for different environments (e.g., development, staging, and production).

It's a good practice to use environment-specific configuration files.

- o **.env files** are commonly used for storing environment variables like API keys, database credentials, and other configuration settings.

3. **Setting Up Databases and External Services**:
   - o Ensure that external services such as APIs, databases, and third-party systems are correctly configured and accessible by the agent in the production environment.
   - o **Example**: Set up and configure a database like **PostgreSQL**, and ensure the agent can read/write to the database as needed.

4. **Testing in a Staging Environment**:
   - o Before moving to production, test the agent in a staging environment that closely mirrors the production system. This helps catch potential issues related to network configurations, database access, and third-party service integrations.

Containerization with Docker

Containerization is the process of packaging the agent along with its environment, dependencies, and configuration into a portable container. **Docker** is a popular platform for creating containers. It ensures that the AI agent will run consistently across different environments.

1. **Creating a Dockerfile**:
   - o A **Dockerfile** is a script that contains instructions on how to build a Docker image, which includes the application and its environment.

   Example Dockerfile for a Python-based AI agent:

```
# Use an official Python runtime as a base image
FROM python:3.8-slim

# Set the working directory inside the container
WORKDIR /app

# Copy the current directory contents into the
container
COPY . /app

# Install the required dependencies
RUN pip install --no-cache-dir -r requirements.txt
```

```
# Set environment variables
ENV ENVIRONMENT=production

# Expose the port that the application will run on
EXPOSE 5000

# Run the agent
CMD ["python", "agent.py"]
```

Explanation:

- The `FROM` instruction specifies the base image (in this case, a Python image).
- The `COPY` command copies the files from the local directory into the container.
- The `RUN` command installs the dependencies specified in `requirements.txt`.
- The `CMD` instruction defines the command to run when the container starts.

2. **Building and Running the Docker Container**:
   - Build the Docker image:
   - `docker build -t my-ai-agent .`
   - Run the container:
   - `docker run -p 5000:5000 my-ai-agent`

This process packages the agent into a container that can be deployed across different systems or cloud platforms.

8.2 Continuous Integration and Continuous Deployment (CI/CD)

CI/CD is a practice that involves automatically testing, building, and deploying software to ensure that new changes are integrated smoothly into the production environment. CI/CD pipelines help streamline the development and deployment processes.

Setting Up CI/CD Pipelines

1. **Continuous Integration**:

- o Continuous integration involves automatically testing new changes (such as code updates) in a staging environment before merging them into the main codebase.
- o Popular CI tools include **Jenkins**, **GitLab CI**, **CircleCI**, and **Travis CI**.

2. **Continuous Deployment**:
   - o Continuous deployment automatically pushes tested code to production without manual intervention, ensuring that updates are delivered quickly.
   - o With CI/CD in place, code changes are automatically built, tested, and deployed as soon as they are committed to the version control system (e.g., Git).

Example CI/CD Workflow:

1. **Code Commit**: Developers commit code to the repository (e.g., on GitHub).
2. **Build Stage**: The CI server builds the application and ensures all dependencies are resolved.
3. **Test Stage**: The CI system runs automated tests to ensure the agent is functioning as expected.
4. **Deploy Stage**: If tests pass, the system automatically deploys the code to production or a staging environment.

Automated Testing and Deployment

Automated testing ensures that the code works as expected. Testing can include:

- **Unit Testing**: Testing individual components or functions.
- **Integration Testing**: Testing the interaction between components.
- **End-to-End Testing**: Testing the entire application from start to finish, simulating real-world scenarios.

For example, in Python, you can use **pytest** for unit testing:

Test Example:

```
def test_agent_function():
    agent = MyAgent()
    result = agent.some_method()
    assert result == expected_value
```

After tests pass, the system automatically deploys the updated agent to production.

8.3 Monitoring and Maintenance

After deploying AI agents to production, it's crucial to monitor their performance and ensure that they remain functional over time. Monitoring helps detect issues early, while maintenance ensures that the agent continues to operate efficiently.

Tools for Monitoring Agent Performance

1. **Logging**:
   - Proper logging provides insights into how the agent is performing in real-time. Logs can include information about actions taken, errors encountered, and performance metrics.
   - **Tools**: **ELK Stack** (Elasticsearch, Logstash, Kibana), **Grafana**, and **Prometheus** are popular tools for monitoring logs and performance metrics.
2. **Performance Metrics**:
   - Key performance metrics to monitor include:
     - **Response Time**: How long it takes the agent to complete a task.
     - **Error Rate**: The frequency of errors or failures.
     - **Uptime**: The percentage of time the agent is operational.
     - **Resource Utilization**: CPU and memory usage of the agent.
3. **Real-Time Monitoring**:
   - Tools like **Datadog** and **New Relic** provide real-time monitoring, allowing you to track your agent's performance and receive alerts if anything goes wrong.

Strategies for Maintenance and Updates

1. **Regular Updates**:
   - Ensure that the agent's software, dependencies, and security patches are up-to-date to maintain security and performance.
2. **Graceful Restart**:

o In case of an issue, a graceful restart can allow the agent to recover without causing downtime. This can be handled automatically using orchestrators like **Kubernetes**.

3. **Backup and Rollback**:
   o Maintain backups of critical data and system configurations. If an update causes issues, you should be able to roll back to a previous version of the agent without disruption.

8.4 Scaling Strategies

As the demand for your AI agent grows, you need to ensure that the system can handle increased traffic and workload. There are two primary types of scaling: **horizontal scaling** and **vertical scaling**.

Horizontal vs. Vertical Scaling

1. **Horizontal Scaling (Scaling Out)**:
   o Involves adding more instances of the agent or application. This allows the system to distribute the load across multiple machines or containers.
   o Example: In a cloud environment, you can scale your agent by increasing the number of running instances in **AWS Elastic Beanstalk** or **Kubernetes Pods**.
2. **Vertical Scaling (Scaling Up)**:
   o Involves adding more resources (CPU, memory) to an existing machine or instance.
   o Example: If the agent is running on a cloud server, you can increase the server's resources to handle more traffic.

Scaling Example with Docker:

You can use **Docker Compose** to deploy multiple instances of your agent:

```
version: '3'
services:
  agent1:
    image: my-ai-agent
    deploy:
      replicas: 3  # Scale to 3 instances
  agent2:
```

```
image: my-ai-agent
deploy:
  replicas: 2  # Scale to 2 instances
```

Load Balancing and Resource Management

1. **Load Balancing**:
   o A **load balancer** distributes incoming traffic evenly across multiple agent instances to ensure no single instance is overwhelmed.
   o Common load balancing services include **AWS Elastic Load Balancer**, **NGINX**, and **HAProxy**.
2. **Resource Management**:
   o Use tools like **Kubernetes** for automated scaling and resource allocation. Kubernetes can manage the deployment of AI agents, automatically scaling them based on demand and ensuring optimal resource usage.

8.5 Emerging Deployment Trends

As the AI landscape evolves, new deployment trends are emerging, enabling agents to be deployed more efficiently and with greater flexibility.

Edge AI Deployments

Edge computing involves processing data closer to the source (e.g., on devices like sensors, mobile phones, or IoT devices) rather than in a centralized cloud environment. This reduces latency and allows real-time processing.

- **Example**: **Edge AI** in autonomous vehicles, where AI agents process sensor data locally to make real-time driving decisions without relying on cloud servers.

Serverless Architectures

In a **serverless architecture**, you don't need to manage the infrastructure. Instead, your AI agent's functions are executed on-demand in response to events. This reduces costs and simplifies scaling.

- **Example**: Deploying your AI agent on **AWS Lambda** or **Google Cloud Functions**, where you only pay for the computation time your agent uses.

Summary

In this chapter, we covered:

- **Preparing for deployment**: Ensuring the environment is configured and using Docker for containerization.
- **CI/CD**: Setting up continuous integration and deployment pipelines to automate the testing and deployment process.
- **Monitoring and maintenance**: Using monitoring tools and strategies for maintaining agent performance.
- **Scaling strategies**: Horizontal and vertical scaling to handle increasing workloads and using load balancing for resource management.
- **Emerging deployment trends**: Edge AI deployments and serverless architectures for more efficient, flexible agent deployment.

By following the steps outlined in this chapter, you can successfully deploy and scale your AI agents to handle real-world demands efficiently, ensuring they perform well and remain secure and up-to-date.

Chapter 9: Security and Compliance in Autonomous AI Systems

As AI systems, especially autonomous agents, are deployed across industries, ensuring their security and compliance becomes critical. Autonomous AI agents often interact with sensitive data and perform actions in real-world environments, which can lead to significant risks if not properly secured. In this chapter, we will examine the security risks that AI systems face, discuss best practices for securing them, explore compliance with regulations such as **GDPR** and **HIPAA**, and highlight the importance of auditing and logging to maintain system integrity and security.

9.1 Understanding Security Risks

AI systems, particularly autonomous agents, are vulnerable to a wide range of security threats. These risks can lead to data breaches, unauthorized access, or malfunction of the AI system, causing harm to users, businesses, or the environment.

Common Threats to AI Systems

1. **Adversarial Attacks**:
   - **Description**: Adversarial attacks involve manipulating the input data to an AI system to fool the agent into making incorrect decisions. For example, an adversarial image might cause a computer vision agent to misclassify objects.
   - **Impact**: This type of attack can lead to poor decision-making by the agent, causing safety risks, such as autonomous vehicles misinterpreting road signs.
   - **Mitigation**: Use adversarial training techniques and robust models to detect and prevent these attacks.
2. **Data Poisoning**:
   - **Description**: In data poisoning, malicious actors manipulate the training data used by the AI system, leading to compromised models that make biased or incorrect predictions.

- o **Impact**: AI agents trained with poisoned data can exhibit harmful behavior, such as misclassification in medical diagnoses or fraud detection systems.
- o **Mitigation**: Regularly audit the training data for anomalies, and use robust data validation techniques.

3. **Model Inversion**:
   - o **Description**: In model inversion attacks, an adversary tries to reverse-engineer the AI model to extract sensitive information, such as private user data used during model training.
   - o **Impact**: Sensitive data can be leaked, exposing personal information and violating privacy.
   - o **Mitigation**: Employ techniques such as differential privacy and secure model storage to prevent model inversion.

4. **Denial-of-Service (DoS) Attacks**:
   - o **Description**: DoS attacks overwhelm an AI system's resources or network, preventing it from functioning properly.
   - o **Impact**: A DoS attack can render an autonomous AI system unresponsive or slow, which can have disastrous consequences, especially in critical systems like healthcare or transportation.
   - o **Mitigation**: Implement network monitoring tools to detect unusual traffic patterns and deploy rate limiting to protect against DoS attacks.

5. **Unauthorized Access**:
   - o **Description**: Unauthorized access occurs when malicious actors gain access to an AI system's internal components or data, either through weak credentials or exploiting vulnerabilities.
   - o **Impact**: Attackers can manipulate the AI system's behavior, access sensitive information, or shut down the system.
   - o **Mitigation**: Implement strong authentication mechanisms, such as multi-factor authentication (MFA), and ensure access control policies are in place.

Case Studies of Security Breaches

1. **Tesla's Autopilot Incident (2016)**:
   - o **Incident**: In 2016, a Tesla vehicle's autopilot feature failed to recognize a white truck against a bright sky, leading to a fatal crash. While not directly a security breach, this highlighted

the risks AI agents face when relying on flawed perception algorithms.

- o **Lessons**: The incident demonstrated the need for robust training and testing of autonomous agents, especially in critical systems like self-driving cars.

2. **DeepMind's AI Health Data Leak (2016)**:
   - o **Incident**: In 2016, it was revealed that DeepMind's AI system for healthcare had accessed sensitive patient data without proper consent, breaching privacy regulations.
   - o **Lessons**: This breach emphasized the importance of complying with privacy regulations like **HIPAA** and ensuring data access is controlled and transparent.

9.2 Implementing Security Best Practices

To protect AI systems from the aforementioned threats, it is crucial to implement security best practices at every stage of development, deployment, and operation.

Authentication and Authorization

1. **Authentication**:
   - o Authentication verifies the identity of users or systems attempting to access the AI system.
   - o **Best Practice**: Implement **multi-factor authentication (MFA)**, where users are required to provide two or more verification factors (e.g., password and biometrics) to gain access.

   Code Example for MFA (Python):

   ```python
   import pyotp  # Install pyotp library for MFA

   # Generate a TOTP (Time-based One-Time Password) secret
   totp = pyotp.TOTP('JBSWY3DPEHPK3PXP')  # Replace with
   your secret key
   print("Current OTP:", totp.now())  # Generates a one-
   time password
   ```

2. **Authorization**:

- o Authorization determines what actions authenticated users or systems can perform.
- o **Best Practice**: Implement **role-based access control (RBAC)**, where users are assigned roles, and each role has specific permissions. This ensures that only authorized users can perform sensitive actions.

Code Example for RBAC (Python):

```python
user_roles = {
    'admin': ['read', 'write', 'delete'],
    'user': ['read'],
}

def check_permission(user_role, action):
    if action in user_roles.get(user_role, []):
        return True
    return False

print(check_permission('admin', 'delete'))  # True
print(check_permission('user', 'delete'))  # False
```

Data Encryption Techniques

Data encryption ensures that sensitive data is protected during storage and transmission. It prevents unauthorized access to data even if attackers gain access to the system.

1. **Encryption at Rest**:
   - o Data stored on servers or databases should be encrypted using **AES (Advanced Encryption Standard)** with a 256-bit key. This ensures that data remains protected even if an attacker gains access to the storage medium.
2. **Encryption in Transit**:
   - o Use **TLS (Transport Layer Security)** to encrypt data transmitted over networks. This protects data from being intercepted or modified during communication.

Code Example for TLS Encryption (Python):

```python
import ssl
import socket

context =
ssl.create_default_context(ssl.Purpose.CLIENT_AUTH)
```

```
connection =
context.wrap_socket(socket.socket(socket.AF_INET),
server_hostname="example.com")
connection.connect(('example.com', 443))
connection.sendall(b"GET / HTTP/1.1\r\nHost:
example.com\r\n\r\n")
print(connection.recv(1024))
```

9.3 Compliance Standards and Regulations

Autonomous AI systems often handle sensitive data, which requires compliance with various privacy and security regulations. These regulations ensure that the data is handled properly and that user rights are protected.

GDPR, HIPAA, and Other Regulations

1. **GDPR (General Data Protection Regulation)**:
   o **Scope**: GDPR applies to companies that collect, store, or process data of individuals in the European Union (EU).
   o **Requirements**:
      ▪ Obtain **explicit consent** from users before collecting personal data.
      ▪ Provide users with the right to access, correct, and delete their data.
      ▪ Implement strong data protection measures to prevent unauthorized access.
2. **HIPAA (Health Insurance Portability and Accountability Act)**:
   o **Scope**: HIPAA governs the use and disclosure of personal health information (PHI) in the United States.
   o **Requirements**:
      ▪ Ensure the **confidentiality** and **security** of PHI.
      ▪ Perform **risk assessments** and ensure **secure data storage** and transmission.
3. **CCPA (California Consumer Privacy Act)**:
   o **Scope**: CCPA applies to businesses that collect personal data of California residents.
   o **Requirements**:
      ▪ Provide consumers with the right to request the deletion of personal data.
      ▪ Offer **opt-out** mechanisms for consumers to stop the sale of their data.

Ensuring Compliance in AI Systems

1. **Data Minimization**:
   o Collect only the data that is necessary for the AI agent's functionality. This reduces the risk of violating privacy regulations and enhances the security of personal data.
2. **User Consent**:
   o Always obtain user consent before collecting any personal or sensitive data. This can be done through explicit opt-ins, and users should be informed of how their data will be used.
3. **Data Anonymization**:
   o Anonymize personal data whenever possible. This can be particularly useful in AI systems that process large datasets to prevent personal data from being exposed.

9.4 Auditing and Logging

Auditing and logging are essential for ensuring transparency and accountability in AI systems. By maintaining detailed logs of system activities, you can detect unusual behavior, investigate security incidents, and comply with regulations.

Implementing Effective Logging Mechanisms

1. **Centralized Logging**:
   o Use centralized logging systems like **ELK Stack** (Elasticsearch, Logstash, Kibana) or **Splunk** to collect and analyze logs from multiple sources. Centralized logging ensures that all events are recorded in one place for easy access.
2. **Log Levels**:
   o Implement different log levels to categorize log entries based on their severity:
     ▪ **INFO**: Routine information.
     ▪ **DEBUG**: Detailed diagnostic information.
     ▪ **ERROR**: Critical errors.
     ▪ **WARNING**: Non-critical issues.

   Code Example for Logging (Python):

```
import logging

logging.basicConfig(level=logging.INFO)

def perform_action():
    logging.info("Action started")
    try:
        # Simulate an error
        x = 1 / 0
    except Exception as e:
        logging.error(f"Error occurred: {e}")

perform_action()
```

Explanation:

- o The code uses Python's `logging` module to record the start of an action and any errors that occur during the process.

Conducting Security Audits

1. **Regular Audits**:
   - o Conduct regular security audits to identify vulnerabilities, ensure compliance with security standards, and assess the effectiveness of security controls.
2. **Penetration Testing**:
   - o Perform penetration testing to simulate potential attacks on your AI system and identify weaknesses before they are exploited by real attackers.
3. **Compliance Audits**:
   - o Ensure that your AI systems comply with relevant data protection regulations by conducting regular compliance audits and maintaining proper documentation.

Summary

In this chapter, we covered:

- **Security Risks**: We explored the common threats to AI systems, including adversarial attacks, data poisoning, and unauthorized access.

- **Security Best Practices**: We discussed the implementation of authentication, authorization, and data encryption techniques to secure AI systems.
- **Compliance Regulations**: We examined key compliance regulations, such as **GDPR**, **HIPAA**, and **CCPA**, and the steps needed to ensure compliance in AI systems.
- **Auditing and Logging**: We highlighted the importance of logging and conducting regular audits to monitor system activity and ensure security.

By implementing the security measures and compliance practices outlined in this chapter, you can help ensure that your autonomous AI systems remain secure, trustworthy, and compliant with the relevant regulations.

Chapter 10: Observability and Monitoring

In this chapter, we will delve into the importance of **observability and monitoring** in AI systems, particularly in autonomous agents. These systems must be continuously observed to ensure they operate efficiently and effectively in dynamic environments. We will explore the key metrics to monitor, the tools and technologies available for monitoring, best practices for logging and alerting, and techniques for analyzing and visualizing data. By the end of this chapter, you will understand how to set up observability for AI systems, ensuring their reliability and performance in production environments.

10.1 Importance of Observability in AI Systems

Observability refers to the ability to monitor, measure, and understand the internal state of a system based on the data it produces. For AI systems, especially autonomous agents, observability is crucial because it allows developers and operators to track performance, detect anomalies, and ensure that the agent is making decisions as expected.

Key Metrics to Monitor

To ensure that AI agents are functioning optimally, you should monitor several key metrics. These metrics help you assess the performance of both the agents and the underlying systems they depend on.

1. **Response Time**:
    o   Measures how long it takes the AI agent to respond to a request or action. A slow response time can indicate performance bottlenecks or issues with the system's processing power.
    o   **Example**: In a customer support chatbot, if the response time is too slow, users may get frustrated, leading to a poor user experience.
2. **Throughput**:
    o   The number of actions or requests processed by the agent over a specific period. High throughput indicates that the agent is efficiently handling its tasks.

    o **Example**: For an autonomous drone system, throughput could refer to the number of flights or tasks completed per hour.

3. **Error Rate**:
    - o The frequency of errors or failures that occur within the system. High error rates indicate that something is wrong, whether it's due to bad data, misconfigurations, or unexpected scenarios.
    - o **Example**: In a recommendation engine, if the error rate is high, it might mean the system is making incorrect recommendations due to poor training or incorrect data.

4. **Resource Utilization**:
    - o Monitors the consumption of system resources such as CPU, memory, and storage. Excessive resource usage can degrade performance or cause system crashes.
    - o **Example**: An AI agent running in a cloud environment that uses excessive CPU may incur unnecessary costs and reduce the efficiency of the overall infrastructure.

5. **State Transitions**:
    - o For AI agents that follow specific state machines, monitoring how they transition between states can help detect unexpected behavior or deadlock situations.
    - o **Example**: In an autonomous vehicle system, monitoring how the agent transitions from "driving" to "parked" ensures that it is making appropriate decisions during operation.

6. **User Interactions**:
    - o Measures the frequency and types of interactions between users and the AI agent. Understanding these interactions can provide insights into how the agent is performing in real-world scenarios.
    - o **Example**: A chatbot might log user questions to detect patterns in what users are asking and adjust its responses accordingly.

Benefits of Comprehensive Observability

1. **Proactive Problem Detection**:
    - o Observability helps identify potential issues before they affect users. By monitoring metrics such as error rates and response times, you can fix problems proactively, reducing downtime and improving user experience.

2. **Improved Performance**:

- o With detailed insights into the performance of AI agents, you can optimize resource usage, reduce latency, and improve throughput. This leads to better overall efficiency and a faster response from the system.

3. **Enhanced Debugging and Troubleshooting**:
   - o Observability allows for faster identification of issues when they arise. By tracking metrics and logs, you can understand the root causes of problems and address them quickly, minimizing disruption to the service.

4. **Compliance and Auditing**:
   - o Many industries require regular audits to ensure that AI systems are operating ethically and legally. Observability provides the necessary data for these audits, ensuring compliance with regulations and standards.

10.2 Tools and Technologies for Monitoring

There are several tools available to help monitor and observe the behavior of AI agents. These tools allow you to collect, analyze, and visualize key metrics that are critical for understanding the system's performance.

Overview of Popular Monitoring Tools

1. **Prometheus**:
   - o **Description**: Prometheus is an open-source monitoring and alerting toolkit designed for reliability and scalability. It is ideal for monitoring systems with dynamic and distributed components.
   - o **Use Case**: Prometheus can be used to monitor an AI system's infrastructure, such as containerized deployments and cloud services, as well as track custom metrics from AI agents.
   - o **Integration**: Prometheus integrates well with Grafana for data visualization.

2. **Grafana**:
   - o **Description**: Grafana is a data visualization platform that integrates with monitoring tools like Prometheus to display real-time data in interactive dashboards.
   - o **Use Case**: Use Grafana to create dashboards that display the performance of your AI agents, including metrics like response time, throughput, and error rates.

3. **Datadog**:
   - **Description**: Datadog is a comprehensive monitoring solution for cloud environments that offers real-time observability across applications, infrastructure, and logs.
   - **Use Case**: Datadog can track performance metrics, monitor log data, and set up custom alerts for your AI agents and underlying systems.
4. **New Relic**:
   - **Description**: New Relic is a cloud-based performance monitoring tool that provides full-stack observability, including infrastructure, application, and user experience metrics.
   - **Use Case**: It is useful for monitoring the performance of AI agents deployed across complex, multi-cloud environments.
5. **OpenTelemetry**:
   - **Description**: OpenTelemetry is an open-source framework for collecting traces, metrics, and logs from applications. It provides a unified approach to monitoring.
   - **Use Case**: OpenTelemetry can be used to instrument AI agent code to collect observability data, which can then be exported to various backend systems like Prometheus or Datadog.

Integrating Monitoring Tools with LangGraph

LangGraph provides built-in integrations with popular monitoring tools. For example, integrating **Prometheus** with LangGraph can provide detailed observability of the agent's performance.

Example Integration with Prometheus:

1. Install Prometheus and Grafana on your system.
2. In your LangGraph-based agent, expose custom metrics via an HTTP endpoint.
3. Use Prometheus to scrape these metrics, and visualize them in Grafana.

Sample Code for Exposing Metrics in LangGraph:

```
from prometheus_client import start_http_server, Gauge
import time

# Define a metric to monitor response time
```

```
response_time_metric = Gauge('agent_response_time_seconds',
'Response time of the AI agent')

def record_response_time():
    start = time.time()
    # Simulate agent action (e.g., processing a request)
    time.sleep(1)  # Sleep for 1 second to simulate
processing
    response_time = time.time() - start
    response_time_metric.set(response_time)

if __name__ == '__main__':
    # Start the Prometheus server
    start_http_server(8000)  # Expose metrics on port 8000
    while True:
        record_response_time()
        time.sleep(5)  # Record every 5 seconds
```

Explanation:

- This code uses the **Prometheus client** library to expose a custom metric (`agent_response_time_seconds`) that measures the time taken for the agent to process requests.
- Prometheus can scrape these metrics and display them on a Grafana dashboard.

10.3 Implementing Logging and Alerting

Logging and alerting are critical components of monitoring that help in detecting and diagnosing issues in AI systems. Logs provide a detailed record of what's happening in the system, while alerts notify the team when something goes wrong.

Best Practices for Logging

1. **Structured Logging**:
   o Log entries should be structured (e.g., JSON format) to facilitate easier parsing and analysis.
   o Example:

```
{
    "timestamp": "2025-01-01T12:00:00Z",
    "level": "ERROR",
    "message": "AI agent failed to process request",
```

```
        "details": {
            "agent_id": "agent_123",
            "error_code": 500
        }
    }
```

2. **Log Levels**:
   - Use appropriate log levels to categorize log entries:
     - **DEBUG**: Detailed diagnostic information.
     - **INFO**: Routine information (e.g., system start, task completion).
     - **WARNING**: Non-critical issues.
     - **ERROR**: Problems that require attention.
     - **CRITICAL**: Severe issues that need immediate action.
3. **Centralized Logging**:
   - Use centralized logging systems (e.g., **ELK Stack**, **Splunk**) to aggregate logs from multiple agents and services. This helps in easier management and analysis of logs.

Code Example for Logging (Python):

```python
import logging

logging.basicConfig(level=logging.INFO)

def perform_action():
    logging.info("Action started")
    try:
        # Simulate an error
        x = 1 / 0
    except Exception as e:
        logging.error(f"Error occurred: {e}")

perform_action()
```

Setting Up Alerting Mechanisms

1. **Threshold-Based Alerts**:
   - Set up alerts that trigger when specific thresholds are exceeded, such as high error rates or slow response times.
   - Example: If the error rate exceeds 5% in the past 10 minutes, an alert is triggered.
2. **Anomaly Detection**:

o Use anomaly detection to identify when performance metrics deviate from their normal patterns. This can be achieved using machine learning or rule-based systems.
o **Example Tools**: Datadog, New Relic, and Prometheus offer built-in anomaly detection features.
3. **Notification Channels**:
   o Alerts can be sent through various channels, including email, SMS, Slack, or even integrated into incident management tools like **PagerDuty**.

10.4 Analyzing and Visualizing Data

Analyzing and visualizing the data collected from monitoring tools is crucial to gaining insights into how AI agents are performing. By creating dashboards and visualizations, you can quickly identify trends, spot anomalies, and make data-driven decisions.

Data Visualization Techniques

1. **Time-Series Graphs**:
   o Use time-series graphs to visualize metrics such as response time, error rates, and system resource utilization over time. This helps in identifying trends, spikes, and patterns.
2. **Heatmaps**:
   o Heatmaps are useful for visualizing spatial data, such as the distribution of agent activity in a geographical area or the performance of an AI system across different regions.
3. **Bar and Pie Charts**:
   o Bar and pie charts can be used to visualize categorical data, such as the distribution of different error types or the percentage of tasks completed successfully by the AI agent.

Example Dashboards for AI Agents

1. **AI Agent Performance Dashboard**:
   o **Metrics**: Response time, throughput, error rate, and resource utilization.
   o **Visualizations**: Time-series graphs for response time, bar charts for error categories, pie charts for user interaction types.

2. **AI System Health Dashboard**:
   o **Metrics**: System health (CPU, memory), uptime, and service status.
   o **Visualizations**: Heatmaps for system health, time-series graphs for resource utilization, and system status indicators.

Summary

In this chapter, we covered:

- **Importance of Observability**: Understanding the need to monitor key metrics such as response time, error rates, and resource utilization to ensure AI agents perform optimally.
- **Monitoring Tools**: Overview of popular tools like Prometheus, Grafana, and Datadog, and how to integrate them with LangGraph for performance tracking.
- **Logging and Alerting**: Best practices for logging AI system events and setting up alerting mechanisms to detect issues proactively.
- **Data Visualization**: Techniques for visualizing performance data, including time-series graphs and dashboards, to gain insights and make data-driven decisions.

By implementing these observability practices, you will be able to monitor your AI agents in real time, detect anomalies, and ensure they perform reliably in production environments. In the next chapter, we will explore advanced topics such as improving agent decision-making with reinforcement learning.

Chapter 11: Optimization and Performance Tuning

In this chapter, we will focus on how to optimize and fine-tune the performance of AI agents. As AI systems grow in complexity and scale, performance bottlenecks can emerge, leading to slower response times, higher resource consumption, and increased operational costs. By identifying and addressing these bottlenecks, optimizing code, and applying advanced techniques, we can significantly improve the efficiency of AI systems. We will cover profiling tools, optimization strategies, cost management, and advanced performance testing, with the goal of ensuring that AI agents operate at their best in production environments.

11.1 Identifying Performance Bottlenecks

Before optimizing an AI system, it is essential to identify where the bottlenecks lie. Performance bottlenecks can occur in many parts of the system, such as the code itself, the data pipeline, or the hardware on which the system is running. The process of identifying these bottlenecks is called **profiling**.

Profiling Tools and Techniques

Profiling involves measuring the performance of your application to pinpoint slow sections of code or system processes. Here are some popular profiling tools and techniques to help identify performance bottlenecks:

1. **CPU Profiling**:
   - **Tools**: Python's **cProfile**, **line_profiler**, and **Py-Spy** are excellent tools to profile CPU usage and identify which functions are consuming the most processing power.

   Example (Python cProfile):

```
import cProfile

def some_function():
    total = 0
    for i in range(1, 1000000):
```

```
        total += i
    return total

cProfile.run('some_function()')
```

Explanation: cProfile will output the time spent in each function call, helping to identify where most of the processing time is spent.

2. **Memory Profiling**:
   o **Tools**: **memory_profiler** and **guppy3** allow you to profile memory usage in Python programs, which can be helpful for identifying memory leaks or inefficient memory allocation.

   Example (Python memory_profiler):

```
from memory_profiler import profile

@profile
def some_function():
    total = 0
    for i in range(1, 1000000):
        total += i
    return total

if __name__ == "__main__":
    some_function()
```

Explanation: By adding the @profile decorator to the function, memory_profiler will track memory usage during execution and output detailed statistics.

3. **Database Profiling**:
   o **Tools**: Use database query analyzers such as **EXPLAIN** in SQL to identify slow-running queries. For NoSQL databases like MongoDB, tools like **MongoDB Atlas** provide performance monitoring.
   o **Tip**: Always check the execution time of queries and ensure that indexes are being used appropriately.
4. **Network Profiling**:
   o **Tools**: For AI systems that interact with external services or APIs, tools like **Wireshark** and **tcpdump** can help monitor network traffic and identify latency issues.
   o **Tip**: Track API response times to ensure that external requests aren't causing delays.

Common Performance Issues in AI Agents

1. **Inefficient Algorithms**:
    o AI agents often use complex algorithms for decision-making, which can be inefficient. For instance, exhaustive search algorithms or non-optimal heuristics may slow down performance.
    o **Solution**: Review algorithm complexity and consider more efficient algorithms or heuristics (e.g., switching from a brute-force search to a greedy or dynamic programming approach).
2. **High Resource Consumption**:
    o AI systems often require significant resources, especially in machine learning tasks. If an agent uses excessive CPU, memory, or network bandwidth, it can affect overall system performance.
    o **Solution**: Optimize code, use caching strategies, and ensure that resource-intensive tasks are offloaded appropriately.
3. **Data Pipeline Bottlenecks**:
    o A slow data pipeline can delay the input/output processing of AI agents. This is particularly relevant for systems that process large datasets in real time.
    o **Solution**: Use parallel processing techniques, optimize data storage and retrieval, and reduce data transformation overheads.

11.2 Optimization Strategies

Once you have identified the performance bottlenecks, you can start optimizing the system to address them.

Code Optimization

1. **Optimizing Algorithms**:
    o **Solution**: Analyze algorithmic complexity (Big-O notation) and improve the efficiency of computational steps. For example, replace nested loops with hash tables or trees for faster lookups.
    o **Example**: If you're sorting a large dataset, replacing a bubble sort with a more efficient sorting algorithm like **quick sort** or **merge sort** can significantly improve performance.

2. **Vectorization**:
   - **Solution**: In Python, **NumPy** and **Pandas** allow for efficient vectorized operations, which are much faster than iterating over lists.

Example (NumPy Vectorization):

```
import numpy as np

# Slow version with a loop
def slow_version(arr):
    result = []
    for num in arr:
        result.append(num ** 2)
    return result

# Fast version with NumPy
def fast_version(arr):
    return np.square(arr)

arr = np.array([1, 2, 3, 4, 5])
print(slow_version(arr))
print(fast_version(arr))
```

Explanation: The NumPy version is much faster because it performs the operation in a vectorized manner rather than looping through each element.

3. **Avoiding Unnecessary Computations**:
   - **Solution**: Cache results of expensive computations that don't change often (e.g., using **memoization** or **LRU caches**).

Example (Memoization in Python):

```
from functools import lru_cache

@lru_cache(maxsize=None)
def expensive_function(x):
    print(f"Computing for {x}")
    return x * x

print(expensive_function(4))
print(expensive_function(4))   # This will use the
cached result
```

4. **Parallelism and Concurrency**:

o **Solution**: Use **multithreading** or **multiprocessing** to execute tasks concurrently, which can speed up processing for independent tasks.

o **Example**: Use the **concurrent.futures** library in Python to execute tasks in parallel.

Resource Allocation and Management

1. **Memory Management**:
   o **Solution**: Minimize memory usage by using memory-efficient data structures (e.g., using **generators** in Python instead of lists for large datasets). Also, periodically check for memory leaks and optimize memory allocation strategies.

   Example (Using Generators):

```
def generate_numbers():
    for i in range(1000000):
        yield i

# Using a generator is more memory-efficient than a
list
for num in generate_numbers():
    if num == 10:
        break
```

2. **Efficient Resource Utilization**:
   o **Solution**: Ensure efficient use of system resources by load balancing and managing resource-intensive operations through queues or batch processing.

11.3 Cost Optimization

AI systems, particularly those running in cloud environments, can incur significant operational costs. Cost optimization ensures that the resources are used efficiently and that you only pay for what you need.

Managing Operational Costs

1. **Serverless Architectures**:
   o **Solution**: Use **serverless** architectures like **AWS Lambda**, **Google Cloud Functions**, or **Azure Functions** for event-driven applications. Serverless computing charges you only for the execution time, helping to reduce costs.
2. **Auto-Scaling**:
   o **Solution**: Use auto-scaling features provided by cloud platforms to automatically scale the infrastructure based on workload demands. This helps avoid over-provisioning and reduces costs.

   Example (AWS Auto-Scaling):

   o You can set up auto-scaling policies to automatically increase or decrease the number of EC2 instances based on CPU usage or other metrics.

Efficient Use of Cloud Resources

1. **Spot Instances**:
   o **Solution**: Use **spot instances** or **preemptible VMs** for non-critical tasks. These instances are typically much cheaper than regular instances but may be terminated by the cloud provider with little notice.
2. **Cost Monitoring Tools**:
   o **Solution**: Use cloud cost monitoring tools such as **AWS Cost Explorer** or **Google Cloud Cost Management** to track and optimize your cloud resource usage and prevent unnecessary expenses.

11.4 Performance Testing

Performance testing is an essential step to assess the scalability, stability, and responsiveness of AI agents in real-world scenarios. It helps identify potential issues before they affect users.

Load Testing and Stress Testing

1. **Load Testing**:
   - o **Solution**: Load testing involves simulating normal usage loads to verify that the AI agent can handle expected traffic and processing volumes.
   - o Tools like **JMeter**, **Gatling**, and **Locust** are often used for load testing.
2. **Stress Testing**:
   - o **Solution**: Stress testing involves pushing the system beyond its limits to identify the breaking point. This helps determine how the AI agent behaves under extreme conditions.

Example (Stress Testing with Locust):

```
from locust import HttpUser, task, between

class AIUser(HttpUser):
    wait_time = between(1, 2)

    @task
    def test_api(self):
        self.client.get("/api/ai_agent")
```

Explanation: This script uses **Locust** to simulate user traffic and test the performance of an AI agent's API under load.

Analyzing Test Results

1. **Throughput and Response Time**:
   - o **Solution**: Measure throughput (requests per second) and response time to evaluate how the system performs under load.
2. **Resource Utilization**:
   - o **Solution**: Monitor system resource usage (CPU, memory, etc.) during performance tests to ensure that the agent can handle the expected load without exceeding available resources.

11.5 Advanced Optimization Techniques

For large-scale AI systems, applying advanced optimization techniques is essential to ensure optimal performance.

Parallel and Distributed Computing

1. **Parallel Computing**:
   o **Solution**: Use parallel computing to break down complex tasks into smaller sub-tasks that can be processed simultaneously, speeding up computation.
   o Tools like **CUDA** (for NVIDIA GPUs) or **OpenMP** can help with parallelizing tasks.
2. **Distributed Computing**:
   o **Solution**: Distribute tasks across multiple machines to handle large-scale computations. Platforms like **Apache Spark** or **Dask** provide tools for distributed computing in Python.

Example (Using Dask for Parallel Computing):

```
import dask.array as da

x = da.random.random((10000, 10000), chunks=(1000, 1000))
y = da.random.random((10000, 10000), chunks=(1000, 1000))
result = x + y
result.compute()
```

Energy Efficiency in AI Systems

1. **Energy-Efficient Hardware**:
   o **Solution**: Use energy-efficient hardware, such as specialized processors (e.g., **TPUs**, **GPUs**), which are designed to handle AI workloads with lower power consumption.
2. **Optimizing Algorithmic Efficiency**:
   o **Solution**: Optimize the algorithms used by AI agents to reduce computational complexity. For example, using pruning or quantization techniques to reduce the size of neural networks can improve both performance and energy efficiency.

Summary

In this chapter, we covered:

- **Identifying Performance Bottlenecks**: Techniques for profiling AI agents and identifying common performance issues.
- **Optimization Strategies**: Approaches for optimizing code, memory usage, and resource allocation to improve the performance of AI agents.
- **Cost Optimization**: Strategies for managing operational costs, especially when using cloud services.
- **Performance Testing**: Methods for load and stress testing to ensure that AI agents perform well under expected and extreme conditions.
- **Advanced Optimization Techniques**: Using parallel and distributed computing, as well as optimizing for energy efficiency in AI systems.

By following these optimization strategies, you can significantly enhance the performance, scalability, and efficiency of your AI agents, ensuring that they operate smoothly and cost-effectively in real-world environments.

Chapter 12: Case Studies and Real-World Applications

In this chapter, we will explore real-world applications of autonomous AI systems through detailed case studies. By examining these case studies, we can better understand how AI agents are deployed to solve complex problems in diverse industries. Each case study will include a problem statement, a solution implementation, and the results and key learnings. Additionally, we will explore other real-world examples from various sectors like healthcare, finance, and retail.

12.1 Case Study 1: AI-Powered Customer Support System

Problem Statement

In today's digital age, businesses are increasingly offering customer support through AI-powered systems to handle large volumes of inquiries. A global e-commerce company faced challenges with its customer support department. Despite having a dedicated team, the company struggled to manage the rising number of customer service tickets and provide quick responses to customers. The system was often overwhelmed by the sheer volume of inquiries, leading to delays in responses, lower customer satisfaction, and high operational costs.

Solution Implementation

The solution was to deploy an AI-powered customer support chatbot, leveraging **Natural Language Processing (NLP)** and **Machine Learning (ML)** to automate responses. The system was designed to handle frequently asked questions (FAQs), troubleshoot common problems, and escalate complex issues to human agents.

1. **System Architecture**:
   o The chatbot was integrated into the company's website and mobile app.

- It used **NLP algorithms** to understand customer queries and match them with predefined answers.
- For escalated queries, the system used **machine learning models** to analyze the complexity of the issue and route it to the appropriate human agent.

2. **Technology Stack**:
- **NLP**: Used libraries like **spaCy** and **NLTK** for text processing and understanding.
- **Machine Learning**: Utilized models trained on historical customer support data to predict the most appropriate responses.
- **Integration**: Integrated the system with existing customer service platforms using APIs to escalate tickets.

3. **Implementation Phases**:
- **Phase 1**: Data collection and training—The system was trained on past customer service interactions to identify patterns and common issues.
- **Phase 2**: Development and integration of the AI chatbot into the customer service workflow.
- **Phase 3**: Real-time monitoring and iteration—The system was continuously improved based on feedback and evolving customer queries.

Results and Learnings

- **Increased Efficiency**: The AI-powered system successfully handled over 70% of customer inquiries without human intervention, drastically reducing the load on human agents.
- **Reduced Response Time**: The average response time dropped from 2 hours to under 5 minutes.
- **Improved Customer Satisfaction**: Customers reported a higher satisfaction rate due to faster responses, leading to improved customer retention.
- **Cost Savings**: The company reduced its customer service operating costs by automating routine inquiries, enabling human agents to focus on more complex cases.

Key Learnings:

- Regularly updating the AI model with new customer queries is crucial to maintaining its effectiveness.

- Proper escalation mechanisms are necessary to ensure complex issues are handled by human agents, ensuring a smooth customer experience.

12.2 Case Study 2: Autonomous Supply Chain Management

Problem Statement

A multinational retailer faced inefficiencies in its supply chain management. The company had a vast network of warehouses, suppliers, and delivery partners, which required manual coordination and real-time inventory management. The lack of real-time data led to stockouts, excess inventory, and delays in product deliveries, ultimately affecting customer satisfaction and operational costs.

Solution Implementation

The company decided to implement an autonomous AI-driven supply chain management system to optimize inventory, predict demand, and automate key tasks such as order fulfillment and supplier coordination.

1. **System Architecture**:
   - **AI-Powered Demand Forecasting**: The system used machine learning models to predict demand patterns based on historical data, seasonal trends, and external factors like promotions.
   - **Autonomous Inventory Management**: Using IoT sensors and AI algorithms, the system monitored stock levels across warehouses in real-time and automatically triggered restocking orders when inventory dropped below a certain threshold.
   - **Automated Logistics Coordination**: The system coordinated between warehouses, suppliers, and delivery partners using AI-powered algorithms to optimize delivery routes and times.
2. **Technology Stack**:
   - **Machine Learning**: **XGBoost** and **Prophet** were used for demand forecasting and optimization.

- o **IoT**: Integrated with IoT devices to track inventory and shipments in real-time.
- o **Robotics**: Autonomous robots were used in warehouses to retrieve and sort products based on incoming orders.

3. **Implementation Phases**:
   - o **Phase 1**: Data collection and model training—The system was trained on historical supply chain data to understand demand patterns and identify inefficiencies.
   - o **Phase 2**: System integration—The AI solution was integrated with the company's existing ERP and warehouse management systems.
   - o **Phase 3**: Testing and fine-tuning—The system was deployed in select warehouses for pilot testing and was gradually scaled.

Results and Learnings

- **Reduced Stockouts and Overstocks**: The system improved inventory management by reducing stockouts by 20% and minimizing excess stock by 15%.
- **Optimized Delivery Routes**: The AI system optimized delivery schedules, reducing transportation costs by 10%.
- **Faster Order Fulfillment**: Warehouse robots and automated systems improved order picking and packing speed, cutting fulfillment time by 30%.
- **Cost Reduction**: Overall, the AI-driven supply chain management system led to a 25% reduction in operational costs.

Key Learnings:

- The quality of data used for training AI models is crucial for achieving accurate demand forecasting and inventory management.
- Regular monitoring and adjustments are necessary to fine-tune the system as the supply chain dynamics change over time.

12.3 Case Study 3: Intelligent Traffic Management

Problem Statement

In a large metropolitan city, traffic congestion had become a major issue, leading to long commute times, increased pollution, and inefficient use of infrastructure. The city's existing traffic management system was based on static traffic signals and manual intervention, which failed to adapt to real-time traffic conditions, especially during peak hours or emergencies.

Solution Implementation

The city adopted an intelligent, AI-driven traffic management system that uses real-time data from sensors, cameras, and traffic signals to adjust traffic flows dynamically.

1. **System Architecture**:
   - **Real-Time Traffic Monitoring**: AI algorithms analyzed data from thousands of traffic sensors and cameras installed at key intersections and roadways to monitor vehicle flow and congestion.
   - **Dynamic Traffic Signals**: The system adjusted traffic signal timings in real-time based on the current traffic conditions, optimizing the flow of vehicles and reducing congestion.
   - **Incident Detection and Management**: The system could detect accidents or roadblocks using image recognition and automatically adjust traffic flow to bypass affected areas.
2. **Technology Stack**:
   - **Computer Vision**: Used cameras and computer vision algorithms to analyze traffic patterns and detect incidents.
   - **Reinforcement Learning**: Implemented RL algorithms to optimize the timings of traffic signals based on real-time data.
   - **Cloud Computing**: Utilized cloud infrastructure to store and process the large amounts of data generated by sensors and cameras in real-time.
3. **Implementation Phases**:

- Phase 1: Installation of sensors and cameras throughout the city to gather data and assess traffic patterns.
- Phase 2: Development and deployment of AI algorithms to dynamically adjust traffic lights and reroute traffic.
- Phase 3: Integration with emergency response systems for real-time incident detection and traffic management.

Results and Learnings

- **Reduced Congestion**: The intelligent traffic management system reduced traffic congestion by 30%, leading to smoother flows and shorter commute times.
- **Improved Emergency Response**: The system's ability to detect accidents and reroute traffic improved emergency response times by 20%.
- **Lower Emissions**: By optimizing traffic flow, the system reduced idle times for vehicles, leading to a decrease in CO_2 emissions.
- **Cost Efficiency**: The system saved the city money by reducing the need for manual traffic management and improving the utilization of existing infrastructure.

Key Learnings:

- Integration of real-time data and machine learning models is essential for creating dynamic systems that adapt to changing conditions.
- Effective collaboration between city infrastructure, AI solutions, and cloud services can lead to impactful improvements in urban management.

12.4 Additional Real-World Examples

In addition to the case studies above, AI systems have been implemented across various industries to solve complex problems and improve operational efficiency.

Healthcare

AI agents are increasingly used in healthcare for **diagnostic support**, **patient management**, and **drug discovery**.

1. **Problem**: Diagnosing medical conditions based on imaging (e.g., radiology, pathology slides) can be time-consuming and prone to human error.
2. **Solution**: AI models, particularly **deep learning**, have been used to analyze medical images and assist radiologists in detecting diseases such as cancer, heart conditions, and more.
3. **Results**: AI-powered diagnostic tools have improved detection accuracy, reduced diagnosis time, and enhanced patient outcomes.

Finance

In the finance sector, AI agents are used for **fraud detection**, **automated trading**, and **customer service**.

1. **Problem**: Detecting fraudulent transactions in real-time across millions of transactions is a challenging task.
2. **Solution**: AI-based fraud detection systems use **machine learning models** to analyze transaction data and identify patterns that could indicate fraud.
3. **Results**: These systems have significantly reduced fraudulent activities, saving financial institutions millions of dollars annually.

Retail

In retail, AI agents help with **inventory management**, **personalized recommendations**, and **dynamic pricing**.

1. **Problem**: Retailers often struggle with managing inventory across large stores and warehouses, leading to stockouts or overstocking.
2. **Solution**: AI systems monitor stock levels in real-time and automatically order new products when inventory runs low, improving efficiency and customer satisfaction.
3. **Results**: These systems have led to better inventory turnover, reduced waste, and improved sales.

Summary

In this chapter, we explored several case studies and real-world applications of autonomous AI systems across various industries:

- **AI-Powered Customer Support System**: Automating customer support with AI chatbots to handle common inquiries, leading to improved efficiency and customer satisfaction.
- **Autonomous Supply Chain Management**: Implementing AI to optimize inventory management and delivery processes, resulting in reduced operational costs and improved efficiency.
- **Intelligent Traffic Management**: Using AI to optimize traffic flow in real-time, reducing congestion, improving emergency response, and lowering emissions.
- **Healthcare, Finance, and Retail**: We discussed how AI is transforming healthcare, finance, and retail by improving decision-making, enhancing customer experiences, and optimizing operations.

These case studies and real-world examples highlight the vast potential of AI agents in solving complex problems and driving innovation across industries.

Chapter 13: Best Practices and Lessons Learned

In this final chapter, we will discuss best practices and the valuable lessons learned from building, deploying, and maintaining autonomous AI systems. Designing robust AI systems, managing AI development projects effectively, and ensuring continuous learning are essential for creating AI solutions that are not only efficient but also ethical, trustworthy, and adaptable. Additionally, we will examine how ethical AI practices play a key role in ensuring fairness, accountability, and trust in AI systems.

13.1 Designing Robust AI Systems

Designing a robust AI system involves developing a solution that is resilient, reliable, and adaptable in the face of changing conditions. Robust design ensures that the system performs well under various scenarios, including edge cases, unexpected inputs, and real-world variations.

Principles of Robust Design

1. **Modularity**:
   - Break down the system into smaller, reusable components. This allows for easier updates, testing, and debugging. Each component should have a clear responsibility and interact with other components through well-defined interfaces.
   - **Example**: In an AI-powered customer service system, the chatbot, NLP model, and ticketing system can be developed as separate modules that work together.
2. **Fault Tolerance**:
   - Design the system to handle failures gracefully. A robust system should be able to recover from errors or unexpected inputs without crashing.
   - **Example**: Implementing automatic retries or fallbacks when an AI agent encounters a temporary network issue or when it fails to process a request.
3. **Scalability**:
   - Ensure that the system can handle increased load or complexity over time. Scalability can be achieved through

horizontal scaling (adding more servers or instances) or vertical scaling (upgrading resources on existing machines).
- o **Example**: AI agents used in an e-commerce platform should be able to handle the traffic spikes during Black Friday sales by automatically scaling the backend infrastructure.

4. **Maintainability**:
   - o Design the system so that it can be easily updated and maintained over time. This includes writing clear documentation, using version control, and adhering to coding standards.
   - o **Example**: In an AI-powered recommendation system, maintainability can be achieved by having well-documented APIs that allow for easy updates to recommendation algorithms.

Common Pitfalls to Avoid

1. **Overfitting Models**:
   - o **Problem**: AI models that are too tightly fitted to training data can perform poorly in real-world scenarios due to lack of generalization.
   - o **Solution**: Regularly evaluate models with real-world or unseen data, and use techniques such as cross-validation to ensure the model generalizes well.
2. **Lack of Transparency**:
   - o **Problem**: AI systems that operate as "black boxes" without transparency can be difficult to debug and explain to stakeholders.
   - o **Solution**: Implement **explainable AI (XAI)** techniques to provide insights into how the model makes decisions.
3. **Ignoring Edge Cases**:
   - o **Problem**: Failing to account for edge cases can lead to unexpected behavior in real-world use.
   - o **Solution**: Test AI systems on a diverse set of scenarios, including edge cases, to ensure robustness.

13.2 Effective Project Management for AI Development

AI development projects are complex and require effective management to ensure they meet objectives, timelines, and quality standards. AI projects often involve multidisciplinary teams, including data scientists, engineers, domain experts, and product managers, which require well-coordinated efforts.

Agile Methodologies

1. **Iterative Development**:
   o Use an **Agile** approach where the project is broken down into smaller sprints, typically lasting 1-2 weeks. Each sprint focuses on delivering a specific feature or set of features.
   o **Example**: For an AI-based fraud detection system, one sprint could focus on collecting and preprocessing data, another on developing a machine learning model, and another on testing and integration.
2. **Continuous Feedback**:
   o Agile encourages regular feedback from stakeholders, ensuring that the development process is aligned with business goals and user needs. In AI projects, this can involve regular model evaluations, testing, and refinement based on real-world feedback.
3. **Flexibility**:
   o The AI development process is dynamic, and it's essential to be flexible to adapt to new findings, changes in technology, or shifts in business objectives.
   o **Example**: If initial experiments with a supervised learning approach do not yield satisfactory results, the team might pivot to reinforcement learning based on feedback and further exploration.

Team Collaboration Tools

1. **Version Control**:
   o Tools like **Git** and **GitHub** help teams manage code versions, collaborate on development, and track changes. This is essential for maintaining code quality and ensuring smooth collaboration among team members.

2. **Project Management Tools**:
   - Tools like **Jira**, **Trello**, and **Asana** help manage tasks, track progress, and assign responsibilities. These tools enable teams to stay organized and ensure that project milestones are met.
3. **Communication Tools**:
   - Communication platforms like **Slack**, **Microsoft Teams**, or **Zoom** are essential for facilitating discussions, brainstorming sessions, and virtual meetings, ensuring seamless communication across the team.

13.3 Continuous Learning and Improvement

AI is a rapidly evolving field, and staying up-to-date with the latest advancements is crucial for creating cutting-edge systems. Continuous learning ensures that AI professionals are aware of new tools, algorithms, and research, which can lead to more efficient and effective AI development.

Keeping Up with AI Advancements

1. **Research Papers**:
   - Regularly read academic papers from conferences like **NeurIPS**, **ICML**, and **CVPR** to stay informed about new algorithms, methodologies, and best practices in AI development.
2. **Online Courses and Tutorials**:
   - Platforms like **Coursera**, **edX**, and **Udacity** offer courses on the latest AI techniques and tools. Regularly completing courses can help AI professionals deepen their expertise and learn new skills.
3. **Industry News**:
   - Follow blogs, newsletters, and online communities (e.g., **arXiv**, **Medium**, **Reddit**) to stay updated on the latest trends, breakthroughs, and developments in AI technology.

Community and Resources

1. **Open Source Projects**:
   - Contribute to or learn from open-source AI projects. Platforms like **GitHub** host thousands of AI projects where

developers can share their work, collaborate with others, and learn from existing codebases.

2. **AI Conferences and Meetups**:
   - o Participate in AI conferences, hackathons, and local meetups. These events offer opportunities to network, collaborate, and learn about the latest trends from leading AI practitioners.
3. **Mentorship and Collaboration**:
   - o Collaborating with experienced mentors and peers in the AI community can provide guidance and accelerate personal and professional growth. Join AI forums or social groups to build connections.

13.4 Ethical AI Practices

Ensuring that AI systems are developed and deployed ethically is critical for their success and acceptance. Ethical AI practices help ensure fairness, transparency, accountability, and trust in AI systems.

Ensuring Fairness and Accountability

1. **Bias Mitigation**:
   - o AI systems are susceptible to biases present in training data. It is essential to detect and mitigate these biases to ensure that the AI systems provide fair outcomes for all users.
   - o **Solution**: Regularly audit training datasets for bias and implement techniques like **re-sampling** or **algorithmic adjustments** to correct for unfair outcomes.
   - o **Example**: In a hiring algorithm, ensure that the model is not biased toward certain demographics, such as gender or ethnicity, by balancing the training data and assessing fairness metrics.
2. **Transparent Decision-Making**:
   - o AI systems should be transparent in how they make decisions, especially when they affect individuals' lives. Implementing **explainable AI (XAI)** allows users to understand the reasoning behind AI-generated decisions.
   - o **Solution**: Use tools like **LIME** (Local Interpretable Model-Agnostic Explanations) and **SHAP** (SHapley Additive exPlanations) to provide insights into the model's decision-making process.

3. **Accountability**:
   - ○ Establish clear accountability for AI system behavior. AI developers, organizations, and stakeholders should take responsibility for the ethical and social implications of AI decisions.
   - ○ **Solution**: Develop an AI governance framework that includes regular audits, reviews, and transparency reports to ensure compliance with ethical guidelines and regulations.

Building Trustworthy AI Systems

1. **Privacy Protection**:
   - ○ AI systems must protect user privacy, especially when handling sensitive data. Techniques such as **differential privacy** ensure that data is anonymized and that individuals cannot be identified from the data used by the AI system.
   - ○ **Solution**: Implement strong data encryption, access controls, and secure data sharing protocols.
2. **Ethical Review**:
   - ○ Before deploying AI systems, especially those in sensitive areas like healthcare, finance, or criminal justice, conduct ethical reviews to assess the potential impact on individuals and society.
   - ○ **Solution**: Set up an AI ethics board within the organization to regularly review and assess the ethical implications of AI deployments.
3. **Collaboration with Stakeholders**:
   - ○ Engage stakeholders, including users, regulators, and ethical boards, throughout the development and deployment phases to ensure that the AI system aligns with societal norms and ethical standards.

Summary

In this chapter, we discussed several important best practices and lessons learned from AI development:

- **Designing Robust AI Systems**: We covered principles of robust AI design, including modularity, fault tolerance, scalability, and maintainability, and highlighted common pitfalls to avoid, such as overfitting and lack of transparency.

- **Effective Project Management**: We explored how Agile methodologies and collaboration tools can improve project management for AI development, ensuring timely delivery and team coordination.
- **Continuous Learning and Improvement**: We discussed how AI professionals can stay updated with the latest advancements through research papers, online courses, and community engagement.
- **Ethical AI Practices**: We examined how to ensure fairness, accountability, and transparency in AI systems, emphasizing the importance of mitigating bias and ensuring privacy protection.

By following these best practices, you can build AI systems that are not only high-performing but also ethical, fair, and trusted by users.

Chapter 14: Future Trends in Autonomous AI Systems

In this final chapter, we will explore the future of autonomous AI systems, focusing on emerging technologies, the evolution of AI agents, ethical considerations, and the potential for future applications. Understanding these trends will help developers and organizations stay ahead of the curve in the rapidly evolving AI landscape, ensuring that they are prepared for the next wave of advancements and challenges.

14.1 Emerging Technologies in AI

AI technology is progressing rapidly, and several emerging technologies are poised to enhance the capabilities of autonomous AI systems. These technologies include quantum computing, Internet of Things (IoT) integration, and edge computing, each offering unique benefits that will shape the future of AI.

Quantum Computing and AI

Quantum computing is an emerging field that has the potential to revolutionize the way AI systems process and analyze data. Unlike classical computers, which rely on binary bits (0s and 1s), quantum computers use **qubits** that can represent multiple states simultaneously, allowing them to perform complex calculations at unprecedented speeds.

1. **Benefits for AI**:
    - **Speed and Efficiency**: Quantum computers could dramatically speed up AI algorithms by performing parallel computations and solving problems that are intractable for classical computers, such as simulating large neural networks or solving optimization problems.
    - **Optimization**: Quantum algorithms can potentially optimize AI models more efficiently, helping improve decision-making in applications like logistics, resource allocation, and financial modeling.
    - **Machine Learning**: Quantum-enhanced machine learning (QML) aims to integrate quantum computing with AI,

enabling faster training of models, improved pattern recognition, and the ability to analyze vast datasets that would be difficult for classical computers to process.

2. **Challenges**:
   - ○ **Current Limitations**: Quantum computing is still in its infancy, and scalable, fault-tolerant quantum systems are not yet widely available. The hardware required for quantum computing is highly sensitive to external interference, making it difficult to implement in practical applications.

3. **Future Outlook**:
   - ○ As quantum hardware improves and quantum algorithms are refined, we can expect AI systems to benefit from breakthroughs in computing power, enabling more complex and efficient autonomous AI solutions.

AI in IoT and Edge Computing

The integration of AI with **Internet of Things (IoT)** devices and **edge computing** is another exciting trend that will shape the future of autonomous AI systems. IoT refers to the network of interconnected devices that communicate with each other and share data. Edge computing involves processing data closer to the source (e.g., on IoT devices themselves or nearby servers) rather than relying on a central cloud server.

1. **Benefits of AI and IoT Integration**:
   - ○ **Real-Time Processing**: AI-powered IoT devices can analyze data in real-time, allowing for faster decision-making without needing to send data to the cloud for processing. For example, an autonomous vehicle can use IoT sensors and AI to make immediate decisions based on real-time traffic and sensor data.
   - ○ **Reduced Latency**: By processing data locally, edge computing reduces latency, which is crucial in applications where timely responses are essential, such as healthcare monitoring or autonomous vehicles.
   - ○ **Energy Efficiency**: Edge computing allows for more energy-efficient AI processing by reducing the need for constant communication with the cloud and relying on local resources.

2. **Applications**:
   - ○ **Smart Cities**: AI and IoT can transform urban management, enabling smart traffic systems, energy-efficient buildings, and real-time waste management.

- o **Healthcare**: Wearable devices with AI capabilities can monitor patient vitals and provide real-time alerts for emergencies, all while processing data on the device itself to avoid delays.
- o **Manufacturing**: AI-powered robots on the factory floor can communicate with IoT devices to monitor machinery, optimize production lines, and predict maintenance needs.
3. **Future Outlook**:
    - o As the number of connected devices grows, we can expect AI to become increasingly integrated with IoT and edge computing, enabling more intelligent, decentralized, and efficient systems.

14.2 The Evolution of AI Agents

As AI technology advances, the capabilities of AI agents are evolving. Next-generation AI agents will be more intelligent, adaptable, and autonomous, capable of performing increasingly complex tasks across a variety of industries.

Next-Generation AI Agent Capabilities

1. **Advanced Decision-Making**:
    - o Future AI agents will have the ability to make complex, context-aware decisions based on a combination of historical data, real-time inputs, and probabilistic reasoning. These agents will be able to handle uncertainty and adapt to changing environments.
    - o **Example**: In healthcare, AI agents will not only assist with diagnoses but will also be able to recommend personalized treatment plans by analyzing vast amounts of patient data, including genetic information and lifestyle factors.
2. **Multimodal Learning**:
    - o Next-generation AI agents will integrate multiple types of data, such as text, images, audio, and video, to make more informed decisions. This **multimodal learning** will allow agents to better understand complex scenarios and interact with the world in a more human-like manner.

- o **Example**: A customer support AI agent will be able to analyze both voice and text conversations to better understand customer sentiments and provide more accurate responses.
3. **Autonomous Collaboration**:
   - o AI agents will work together autonomously to complete complex tasks that require collaboration. This will involve communication and coordination between agents to achieve a common goal.
   - o **Example**: In a manufacturing environment, multiple robots equipped with AI will collaborate to assemble products, using real-time data to adjust their movements and processes based on the actions of other robots.
4. **Ethical Decision-Making**:
   - o Future AI agents will be designed to operate within ethical frameworks, making decisions that align with societal norms and values. This will require integrating ethics into the AI training process and ensuring that agents can explain their reasoning.
   - o **Example**: Autonomous vehicles will make decisions in real-time based on ethical principles (e.g., minimizing harm in unavoidable accident scenarios) while ensuring compliance with traffic laws and human safety.

Integration with Other AI Technologies

AI agents will increasingly integrate with other AI technologies such as **natural language processing (NLP)**, **computer vision**, **reinforcement learning**, and **robotics** to create more advanced, adaptive, and intelligent systems.

1. **AI and NLP**: The integration of **deep learning** and **NLP** will allow AI agents to understand and generate human language with greater fluency and accuracy, making them more useful in applications like customer service, content generation, and virtual assistants.
2. **AI and Computer Vision**: Combining AI agents with computer vision will enable them to understand the visual world and make decisions based on visual inputs. This is crucial for applications such as autonomous vehicles, industrial inspection, and security systems.
3. **AI and Robotics**: AI agents integrated with robotic systems will enable machines to perform complex tasks autonomously, such as assembling products, performing surgery, or navigating unfamiliar environments.

14.3 Ethical Considerations and AI Governance

As AI becomes more powerful, it is crucial to ensure that it is developed and used responsibly. Ethical AI practices are vital to ensuring that AI systems are fair, transparent, and aligned with human values.

Ethical AI Development

1. **Fairness**:
   - AI systems must be designed to avoid biases that could lead to unfair treatment of individuals or groups. This includes ensuring that training data is representative and that models are regularly audited for bias.
   - **Example**: A hiring algorithm should be trained with diverse data to prevent discrimination against any gender, ethnicity, or age group.
2. **Transparency and Explainability**:
   - AI systems should be transparent in how they make decisions. **Explainable AI (XAI)** ensures that users and developers can understand the reasoning behind AI-driven decisions.
   - **Example**: A credit scoring AI should explain the factors that contributed to a particular credit score, allowing users to understand how their data was used.
3. **Privacy**:
   - AI systems must protect user privacy and adhere to privacy regulations such as **GDPR** and **CCPA**. This includes ensuring that sensitive data is anonymized and stored securely.
   - **Example**: In healthcare, AI systems must protect patient data and comply with **HIPAA** regulations while processing and analyzing medical records.

Governance Frameworks

1. **AI Ethics Boards**:
   - Organizations should establish AI ethics boards or committees to oversee the development and deployment of AI systems, ensuring that they align with ethical guidelines and regulatory standards.
2. **Regulatory Oversight**:

- Governments and regulatory bodies will play a crucial role in ensuring that AI systems are developed and used responsibly. This will include creating standards and guidelines for AI development, usage, and accountability.
3. **Accountability and Audits**:
   - Regular audits of AI systems are necessary to ensure that they are operating ethically. This includes auditing both the data used for training and the decisions made by the AI system.
   - **Example**: An autonomous vehicle company may conduct regular audits of its AI system to ensure that the vehicle's decision-making process adheres to ethical principles.

14.4 Future Applications and Innovations

AI is evolving rapidly, and its future applications are boundless. Below are some areas where we can expect innovations in autonomous AI systems.

Predicting Future Use Cases

1. **Healthcare**:
   - AI will revolutionize healthcare by improving diagnosis accuracy, personalizing treatments, and enhancing drug discovery. AI agents could assist doctors by analyzing medical images and historical health data to provide accurate, real-time diagnoses and treatment recommendations.
   - **Example**: AI-driven robotic surgeries, where autonomous robots perform delicate operations with precision, reducing recovery times and improving outcomes.
2. **Autonomous Vehicles**:
   - The future of transportation lies in self-driving cars, drones, and other autonomous vehicles. AI will continue to improve the safety, efficiency, and reliability of these systems by enabling real-time decision-making in dynamic environments.
3. **Smart Cities**:
   - AI will play a central role in building smart cities by optimizing traffic management, energy use, and public services. Autonomous agents will work together to monitor city systems and adjust in real-time to improve the quality of life for residents.

Innovations on the Horizon

1. **AI and Quantum Computing**:
   - The integration of AI with quantum computing will lead to breakthroughs in machine learning, optimization problems, and data analysis, enabling AI systems to solve more complex problems faster than

ever before.

2. **Human-AI Collaboration**:
   - Future AI systems will be designed to collaborate with humans rather than replace them. This includes AI assistants that work alongside humans in creative fields, scientific research, and decision-making.
   - **Example**: AI tools that assist scientists in discovering new drugs or help architects design sustainable buildings using AI-driven simulations.

Summary

In this chapter, we discussed the future of autonomous AI systems, including:

- **Emerging Technologies in AI**: The potential impact of quantum computing, IoT, and edge computing on the future of AI.
- **The Evolution of AI Agents**: The next generation of AI agents, including advanced decision-making, multimodal learning, and autonomous collaboration.
- **Ethical Considerations and AI Governance**: The importance of ethical AI development, fairness, transparency, and governance frameworks to ensure responsible AI usage.
- **Future Applications and Innovations**: Predictions for the use of AI in healthcare, autonomous vehicles, and smart cities, as well as upcoming innovations like AI-powered quantum computing and human-AI collaboration.

These future trends will shape the evolution of AI systems, driving innovation and ensuring that AI technologies are developed responsibly and ethically, with the potential to transform industries and society.

Chapter 15: Appendices

This chapter provides additional resources and helpful tools to support your learning and implementation of the concepts covered in the book. It includes a glossary of terms to clarify key concepts, a list of additional resources for further reading, access to sample code examples, a troubleshooting guide, and an index for easy reference.

A.1 Glossary of Terms

This glossary provides clear and concise definitions of key terms and concepts used throughout this book. Familiarizing yourself with these terms will help deepen your understanding of the topics and facilitate smoother communication when working with AI and autonomous systems.

1. **AI (Artificial Intelligence)**:
   o The simulation of human intelligence processes by machines, particularly computer systems. These processes include learning, reasoning, problem-solving, perception, and language understanding.
2. **Autonomous System**:
   o A system that can perform tasks and make decisions without human intervention. Autonomous systems use AI and sensors to interact with their environment and achieve their objectives.
3. **NLP (Natural Language Processing)**:
   o A branch of AI that focuses on the interaction between computers and human language. NLP enables machines to understand, interpret, and generate human language, such as in chatbots and voice assistants.
4. **Machine Learning (ML)**:
   o A subset of AI that involves the use of algorithms and statistical models that allow systems to learn from and make predictions based on data without being explicitly programmed.
5. **Reinforcement Learning (RL)**:

- o A type of machine learning where an agent learns to make decisions by receiving rewards or penalties based on its actions within an environment. This technique is often used for training autonomous systems.
6. **Quantum Computing**:
   - o A type of computing that uses quantum-mechanical phenomena, such as superposition and entanglement, to perform computations. Quantum computing has the potential to solve problems that are infeasible for classical computers.
7. **IoT (Internet of Things)**:
   - o The network of physical devices embedded with sensors, software, and other technologies that connect and exchange data over the internet. IoT devices can include anything from smart home devices to industrial machines.
8. **Edge Computing**:
   - o A distributed computing framework where data processing occurs closer to the source of data (such as IoT devices) rather than being sent to a centralized cloud server. This reduces latency and bandwidth usage.
9. **Explainable AI (XAI)**:
   - o AI systems designed to provide clear and understandable explanations for their decisions, making it easier for users to trust and validate the AI's behavior.
10. **Bias in AI**:

- Bias in AI refers to systematic errors that lead to unfair or discriminatory outcomes, often arising from biased training data or biased algorithms.

A.2 Additional Resources

This section provides a list of books, articles, and online courses to help you further explore the topics covered in this book. These resources will enable you to deepen your knowledge and stay up-to-date with the latest developments in autonomous AI systems.

Books

1. **"Artificial Intelligence: A Modern Approach" by Stuart Russell and Peter Norvig**:

o   A comprehensive textbook on AI that covers the
    fundamentals, algorithms, and applications of AI. It's widely
    used in AI courses and is a must-read for anyone interested in
    the field.
2. **"Deep Learning" by Ian Goodfellow, Yoshua Bengio, and Aaron Courville**:
   o   This book offers an in-depth understanding of deep learning,
       one of the most important subfields of machine learning. It
       covers theory, algorithms, and practical applications of deep
       learning.
3. **"Reinforcement Learning: An Introduction" by Richard S. Sutton and Andrew G. Barto**:
   o   A definitive resource for understanding reinforcement
       learning (RL). It provides both theoretical background and
       practical examples of RL algorithms.

Articles

1. **"The Malicious Use of Artificial Intelligence: Forecasting, Prevention, and Mitigation"**:
   o   This article explores the potential risks and ethical
       considerations related to the use of AI, particularly in
       malicious contexts.
2. **"The Ethics of Artificial Intelligence" by Nick Bostrom and Eliezer Yudkowsky**:
   o   A seminal paper that addresses the ethical challenges of AI,
       focusing on issues such as AI safety, value alignment, and the
       impact of AI on society.

Online Courses

1. **"Machine Learning by Andrew Ng" on Coursera**:
   o   A highly recommended introductory course on machine
       learning, taught by Andrew Ng, that covers basic algorithms,
       data handling, and supervised and unsupervised learning
       techniques.
2. **"AI for Everyone" by Andrew Ng on Coursera**:
   o   A beginner-friendly course that introduces AI concepts
       without requiring prior technical knowledge. It focuses on
       how AI can be implemented across industries and in real-
       world applications.
3. **"Deep Learning Specialization" on Coursera**:

o   A series of five courses that dive deep into deep learning, covering neural networks, convolutional networks, and sequence models, along with practical coding exercises.

A.3 Sample Code Repository

Throughout this book, we have provided various code examples that demonstrate the principles and techniques of autonomous AI systems. To help you implement these concepts on your own, we have made the full set of code examples available in a repository.

Accessing the Complete Code Examples

The complete code examples, including those from this book, are available on **GitHub**. You can access the repository and download the code to experiment with it in your local development environment.

- **GitHub Repository Link**: [GitHub Repo URL]
- **Contents**:
    o   **Folder 1: Basic AI Agents** - Code for creating basic AI agents, including examples of decision-making algorithms and state management.
    o   **Folder 2: Reinforcement Learning Agents** - Code for training and evaluating reinforcement learning agents.
    o   **Folder 3: Multi-Agent Systems** - Code for developing multi-agent systems, focusing on coordination, collaboration, and conflict resolution.
    o   **Folder 4: Real-World Applications** - Complete implementations of AI agents used in applications like customer support and traffic management.

The repository also includes detailed instructions for setting up the development environment, running the code, and modifying it for your own use cases.

A.4 Troubleshooting Guide

When working with AI systems, you may encounter various issues related to code, performance, or integration. This troubleshooting guide addresses some common problems and provides solutions to help you resolve them.

Common Issues and Solutions

1. **Problem: Model Overfitting**
   o **Solution**: Overfitting occurs when the model performs well on training data but poorly on unseen data. To resolve this, try techniques such as cross-validation, early stopping during training, or using regularization (e.g., L2 regularization).
2. **Problem: Slow Inference or Training Times**
   o **Solution**: Slow performance can be caused by inefficient algorithms, large model sizes, or inadequate hardware. Try optimizing the model (e.g., by reducing its complexity), utilizing batch processing, or running the code on a machine with better processing power (e.g., using GPUs).
3. **Problem: Data Quality Issues**
   o **Solution**: Poor data quality can lead to incorrect or biased predictions. Ensure your dataset is clean by removing duplicates, handling missing values, and normalizing or standardizing the data as needed.
4. **Problem: Insufficient Model Explainability**
   o **Solution**: If your model is too complex to explain, consider using explainable AI techniques like LIME or SHAP to understand how the model makes decisions, or switch to more interpretable models like decision trees if feasible.
5. **Problem: Integration Failures**
   o **Solution**: When integrating AI agents into larger systems, ensure that all dependencies are correctly installed and that the data pipeline is properly configured. Use logging and error handling to identify where the integration fails and check the API documentation for compatibility issues.

A.5 Index

The index is a helpful tool for quickly finding specific topics, terms, or sections within the book. Use it to locate definitions, examples, code snippets, and key concepts mentioned throughout the chapters.

Summary

In this chapter, we covered:

- **Glossary of Terms**: Definitions of essential AI and autonomous system concepts.
- **Additional Resources**: A list of books, articles, and online courses to help you further your AI knowledge.
- **Sample Code Repository**: Access to the complete set of code examples from the book, hosted on GitHub.
- **Troubleshooting Guide**: Solutions to common issues encountered when building and deploying AI systems.
- **Index**: A reference tool to easily navigate through the topics in this book.

By using the resources and troubleshooting guide provided in this chapter, you can further enhance your skills, resolve common issues, and dive deeper into the world of autonomous AI systems.

Chapter 16: Exercises and Projects

This chapter is designed to provide you with practical exercises, hands-on projects, and challenges to solidify your understanding of autonomous AI systems. It will help you transition from theoretical knowledge to real-world applications, guiding you through step-by-step implementations, testing your knowledge with practice problems, and providing opportunities to push your skills to the next level with advanced challenges and capstone projects. By the end of this chapter, you will have a deeper understanding of how to apply the concepts learned throughout the book in real-world scenarios.

16.1 Hands-On Projects

Hands-on projects are an excellent way to practice and apply the concepts you've learned. These projects will provide you with real-world scenarios where you can build your own AI agents, integrating the techniques and algorithms covered in the book.

Step-by-Step Project Guides

1. **Building a Basic Customer Support Chatbot**
   o **Objective**: Create a simple AI-powered customer support chatbot that can answer common queries and escalate complex issues to human agents.
   o **Technologies Used**: Natural Language Processing (NLP), Python, spaCy, and Flask for web deployment.

   Steps:

   o **Step 1**: Install and set up the necessary libraries (`spaCy`, `Flask`, `nltk`).
   o **Step 2**: Preprocess customer queries by cleaning the text data (e.g., removing stop words, punctuation, and performing tokenization).
   o **Step 3**: Train a simple NLP model using a predefined dataset of customer queries and responses.
   o **Step 4**: Implement a Flask web server to allow users to interact with the chatbot in real-time.

      o **Step 5**: Add a fallback mechanism that redirects complex queries to a human agent.

Example Code (Basic Chatbot):

```
from flask import Flask, request
import spacy

app = Flask(__name__)
nlp = spacy.load('en_core_web_sm')

@app.route('/chat', methods=['POST'])
def chat():
    user_input = request.json['message']
    doc = nlp(user_input)
    response = "I'm here to help! What can I assist you
with?"
    return {'response': response}

if __name__ == '__main__':
    app.run(debug=True)
```

2. **Building an Autonomous Supply Chain Agent**
      o **Objective**: Develop an autonomous AI agent that optimizes inventory management by predicting stock levels and automatically ordering new stock.
      o **Technologies Used**: Python, machine learning (ML), scikit-learn, time series forecasting.

Steps:

      o **Step 1**: Collect historical data on inventory levels, sales, and lead times.
      o **Step 2**: Clean and preprocess the data for use in machine learning models.
      o **Step 3**: Build a time series forecasting model to predict future demand (e.g., using ARIMA or XGBoost).
      o **Step 4**: Develop an agent that automatically places orders when stock levels drop below a threshold.
      o **Step 5**: Test the system using simulated data to ensure the agent makes accurate predictions and orders.

Example Code (Time Series Forecasting with ARIMA):

```
import pandas as pd
```

```
from statsmodels.tsa.arima.model import ARIMA

# Load historical inventory data
data = pd.read_csv('inventory_data.csv')

# Fit ARIMA model
model = ARIMA(data['stock_level'], order=(5,1,0))
model_fit = model.fit()

# Make forecast for the next period
forecast = model_fit.forecast(steps=1)
print(f"Predicted stock level for next period:
{forecast}")
```

Building Your Own AI Agents

In addition to the above projects, building your own AI agents from scratch will give you a deeper understanding of the design and implementation of autonomous systems.

1. **Autonomous Traffic Management Agent**:
   o **Objective**: Create an AI agent that can optimize traffic light timings based on real-time traffic data.
   o **Technologies Used**: Reinforcement learning, Python, OpenAI Gym (for simulation).

   Steps:

   o **Step 1**: Implement an environment using OpenAI Gym where the AI agent can interact with simulated traffic lights.
   o **Step 2**: Use reinforcement learning (e.g., Q-learning or Deep Q-Networks) to train the agent to optimize traffic light timings based on the flow of traffic.
   o **Step 3**: Test the agent in a variety of simulated traffic conditions to evaluate its performance.

   Example Code (Reinforcement Learning Setup with OpenAI Gym):

```
import gym
import numpy as np

env = gym.make('TrafficManagement-v0')
state = env.reset()
done = False
total_reward = 0
```

```
while not done:
    action = np.random.choice([0, 1, 2])  # Random
traffic light action
    next_state, reward, done, info = env.step(action)
    total_reward += reward
    state = next_state

print(f"Total reward: {total_reward}")
```

16.2 Practice Problems

Testing your knowledge through practice problems is essential to reinforcing your understanding. Below are several problems based on the concepts covered in this book, with a focus on building intuition and improving problem-solving skills.

Questions to Test Your Understanding

1. **Q1: What is the difference between supervised and unsupervised learning in machine learning?**
   - **Answer**: Supervised learning involves training a model using labeled data, where the input data and corresponding output labels are provided. Unsupervised learning, on the other hand, involves learning patterns from data without labeled outputs, such as clustering or dimensionality reduction.
2. **Q2: Describe the role of reinforcement learning in autonomous systems.**
   - **Answer**: Reinforcement learning is a type of machine learning where an agent learns to make decisions by interacting with an environment and receiving feedback in the form of rewards or penalties. It is widely used in autonomous systems, such as robots or self-driving cars, where the agent must learn from its actions over time to maximize rewards.
3. **Q3: How can you mitigate bias in AI models?**
   - **Answer**: Bias in AI models can be mitigated by ensuring diverse, representative training data, regularly auditing models for fairness, using techniques like adversarial training, and applying fairness constraints to the model.
4. **Q4: What are the challenges in deploying autonomous AI systems at scale?**
   - **Answer**: Challenges include handling real-time decision-making, ensuring scalability and fault tolerance, maintaining

data privacy, managing computational resources efficiently, and ensuring system security and robustness under varying conditions.

Solutions and Explanations

1. **Q1 Solution**:
   - Supervised learning is often used for classification and regression tasks, where the goal is to learn a mapping from input data to labeled outputs. Unsupervised learning is used for tasks like clustering, where the goal is to group similar data points without predefined labels.
2. **Q2 Solution**:
   - In reinforcement learning, agents learn optimal behaviors by exploring and exploiting their environment. Autonomous systems like robots and drones can learn complex behaviors through trial and error, using feedback to improve their actions.
3. **Q3 Solution**:
   - Bias mitigation involves checking for biases in the dataset (e.g., demographic or representation biases) and ensuring algorithms are not inadvertently reinforcing them. Techniques like re-sampling data, adjusting the learning process, or applying fairness constraints to the model can help mitigate these biases.
4. **Q4 Solution**:
   - Scaling autonomous AI systems involves ensuring they can handle large volumes of data and interactions. It requires optimizing the underlying infrastructure, employing techniques like edge computing for real-time processing, and ensuring the system can adapt to increasing complexity over time.

16.3 Challenges for Advanced Learners

For those looking to push their skills further, these challenges will allow you to solve more complex problems, integrate multiple AI techniques, and deepen your understanding of autonomous AI systems.

Complex Problems to Solve

1. **Challenge 1: Build a Multi-Agent System for Collaborative Task Completion**
   - **Problem**: Design and implement a multi-agent system where several autonomous agents collaborate to complete a complex task (e.g., package delivery, assembly line).
   - **Goal**: Implement communication protocols and conflict resolution strategies. Use techniques like **game theory** or **negotiation algorithms** to allow agents to cooperate effectively.
2. **Challenge 2: Develop an AI System for Predictive Maintenance**
   - **Problem**: Build an AI-powered system that predicts when machines or devices in a manufacturing plant will fail based on sensor data.
   - **Goal**: Use time series forecasting and anomaly detection to build a model that can predict failures before they occur, minimizing downtime and improving maintenance efficiency.

Enhancing Existing Projects

1. **Challenge 3: Enhance the Traffic Management Agent with Reinforcement Learning**
   - **Problem**: The basic traffic management agent uses static rules. Improve this by implementing reinforcement learning techniques to dynamically optimize traffic light timings based on real-time traffic data.
   - **Goal**: Improve the agent's decision-making by implementing Q-learning or deep Q-networks (DQN) to handle more complex scenarios with larger state spaces.
2. **Challenge 4: Improve the Customer Support Chatbot with Deep Learning**
   - **Problem**: The basic chatbot only uses rule-based responses. Enhance it by implementing a deep learning model (e.g., transformer-based models) for more dynamic and context-aware responses.
   - **Goal**: Train the chatbot using real customer service conversations to improve its

conversational abilities, context retention, and user engagement.

16.4 Capstone Projects

Capstone projects are comprehensive assignments that integrate multiple concepts and techniques learned throughout the book. These projects simulate real-world challenges and provide a holistic learning experience.

Comprehensive Projects Integrating Multiple Concepts

1. **Capstone 1: Autonomous Delivery System**
   - **Objective**: Design an autonomous delivery system where agents navigate an environment, detect obstacles, and optimize their delivery routes.
   - **Technologies Used**: Reinforcement learning, computer vision, multi-agent systems, IoT sensors.
   - **Steps**:
     - Implement a reinforcement learning agent for navigation.
     - Integrate computer vision for obstacle detection.
     - Use IoT sensors for real-time environmental data.
2. **Capstone 2: AI-Powered Financial Trading System**
   - **Objective**: Develop an AI-based trading agent that can make buy or sell decisions based on market data and financial indicators.
   - **Technologies Used**: Machine learning, time series analysis, reinforcement learning.
   - **Steps**:
     - Collect historical financial data for training.
     - Build and train a model using reinforcement learning to maximize returns.
     - Backtest the model against real market data and evaluate performance.

Industry-Specific Challenges

1. **Healthcare: AI for Diagnostic Assistance**
   - **Objective**: Build an AI agent that assists doctors by analyzing medical images (e.g., X-rays, MRIs) to detect diseases.
   - **Technologies Used**: Convolutional neural networks (CNNs), computer vision, deep learning.
2. **Retail: Personalized Recommendation System**

- o **Objective**: Design a recommendation system that provides personalized product recommendations based on user preferences and browsing history.
- o **Technologies Used**: Collaborative filtering, content-based filtering, deep learning.

Summary

In this chapter, we have provided you with:

- **Hands-On Projects**: Step-by-step guides to building your own AI agents and applying key concepts such as NLP, reinforcement learning, and computer vision.
- **Practice Problems**: A series of questions to test your understanding of the material, along with solutions and explanations.
- **Challenges for Advanced Learners**: Complex problems and enhancements for more experienced learners to solve, encouraging the integration of multiple AI techniques.
- **Capstone Projects**: Comprehensive, real-world-inspired projects that simulate actual industry challenges, helping you apply your knowledge in practical settings.

By completing these exercises and projects, you will gain practical experience in designing, implementing, and refining autonomous AI systems, further preparing you for real-world AI applications.